COLOUR
OUTSIDE

COLOUR OUTSIDE

TOM PORTER

THE ARCHITECTURAL PRESS : LONDON

First published in 1982 by
The Architectural Press Limited,
9 Queen Anne's Gate, London SW1H 9BY.

British Library Cataloguing
in Publication Data
Porter, Tom
Colour outside.
1. Color in architecture
I. Title
729'.4 NA2795

ISBN 0 85139 772 7

Typeset by Phoenix Photosetting, Chatham

Printed in Great Britain by
Jolly & Barber Limited, Rugby, Warwickshire

Acknowledgements

The author would like to express his gratitude to all those designers and architects who have graciously contributed material and ideas, and also to thank the following who provided invaluable assistance throughout the preparation of this book: Giovanni Brino, Juan Diaz-Lameda, Luise Margolies de Gasparini, Martin Gordon, Patrice Goulet, John Hanna, Kathleen Hanna, Steen Heidemann-Werner, Ron Hess, Nigel Hiscock, Preben Holst, Mike Jenks, Ian Latham, Jean-Philippe Lenclos, Philip Mclean, Bebbe Klatt Mooring, Ann Osteen, Yehiel Rabinowitz, Fabio Rieti, Adele Shainblum, Peter D. Stone, William Taylor, Jenny Towndrow, Karen Wheeler.

The author acknowledges a special debt to the vigilance of Jack Widgery and C. Roger Harrison of Imperial Chemical Industries Limited; to the expert criticism of H. L. Gloag; and to Sue Goodman, who produced all the line diagrams.

CONTENTS

FOREWORD

by R C Hampel, Chairman, ICI Paints Division

To anyone who works with colour, its importance and potential power are self-evident. It can seem to defy the laws of physics to alter the appearance of size, shape and form. The colour of our surroundings can change our perception of time, some colour combinations making it seem to pass quickly while others have the opposite effect. In skilled hands, colour can influence mood and behaviour: it has the ability to stimulate or relax, cheer or depress. In addition to its more obvious decorative effects, colour can be used to denote boundaries or stamp a signature on a building.

To the initiated, colour can be a powerful psychological tool, and yet on another level it is so much a part of everyday life that we tend to take it for granted. Almost everything we buy, make or grow, is coloured. Try to imagine a world without colour—it makes a very bleak prospect.

Colour has always fascinated man. Our Paleolithic ancestors adorned their caves with red and yellow ochre and mud pigments. Through the centuries in successive empires and cultures, architects have used colour lavishly on their great buildings. The awe-inspiring architecture of ancient Egypt, the Parthenon, Buddhist temples, mosques of the Islamic Empire, Mayan cities in the rain forests of South America and the cathedrals of medieval Europe were all richly adorned with colour. Historically the monochromatic grey stone public buildings of the modern western world are an anomaly.

Today there is a renewed interest in the potential of outside colour as a dimension of architectural design. Tom Porter is one of the champions of this cause and in this book he presents the case most effectively.

I am personally pleased that ICI's Dulux Trade Group is associated with the project. This is, of course, partly because colour is our business, but also because it is my own belief that a greater consideration of the use of colour in that element of the environment constructed by man will do much to make our towns and cities better places in which to live.

R. C. Hampel

INTRODUCTION

by Michael Graves, architect

One can think of the meanings ascribed to colour as being derived primarily from associations found in nature. These associations are for the most part simple and somewhat commonplace. In fact, it could be said that if colour is not understood easily, we run the risk of making levels of abstraction which leave the associative realm and quickly become private or introverted.

What one might call normal associations of colour and material, found in construction and in nature, include red or terra cotta for brick, cream or ranges of white for limestone, travertine, etc., ranges of green for the general landscape, blue for sky, and so on. It is within this deliberately simple range that we start to identify the placement of such associative colour values with that of form itself.

In a time when craft, material and form were understood in a more direct manner, such as in the Romanesque era or in elements of most vernacular construction, there was a one-to-one pairing of material and its colour range. However, at times like the present where we do not count on building out of 'real stuff' but rely on the synthetic, the simulated, and more economical material, we have perhaps three choices: one, we can leave this material in its 'natural' state; two, we can apply painted or stained surfaces or other decorative coverings to the material in an abstract, intuitive, or personal way; or three, we can, through painting and other coverings, identify the forms and materials that we use with associations that allow interpretations and allusions not given by the first two options.

In exploring the second and third option, the author shows how colour, as both an abstract and a descriptive element, can enrich the form of space with greater significance than a more neutral position would allow.

Michael Graves

1 THE LOST HUES

Today, architects and designers all over the world are showing a renewed interest in the role of colour in all aspects of design, but particularly in its place in the creation of the built environment. The potential of outside colour seems fresh and promising if only because two decades ago the subject was not seriously raised. Throughout history certain generations—such as our own—seem to have to rediscover the potentialities of outside colour, but perhaps never with greater passion than when the early archaeologists unearthed the unsuspected truth about the great monuments of antiquity.

It was during the mid-eighteenth century that, to the horror of the more purist classicists and artists, archaeologists began to announce their discovery of fragments of buildings which were either stained or coated with layers of bright pigment. Others were beginning to publish their discovery that Greek statues and temples had flecks of paint on them. Their descriptions corrected a common misconception that the plastic works of the ancients were simply essays in form and space—articulated by a reverence for the inherent appearance of natural materials. C. W. Ceram perhaps best illustrates the ancient Greek predilection for applied colour: 'Statuary was deeply dyed with garish pigments. The marble figure of a woman found on the Athenian Acropolis was tinctured red, green, blue and yellow. Quite often statues had red lips, glowing eyes made of precious stones and even artificial eyelashes.'

The outcry which followed such findings is not surprising, for the remnants of ancient civilizations, having survived the ravages of time above ground (but bleached of their original colouring), had functioned as monochromatic sources of inspiration—three-dimensional models in stone to be emulated and even imitated by architects down the ages. Meanwhile, those buried underground by the action of man-made and natural forces had

1.2

become suspended in time awaiting their moment to be discovered. Again, an unknown author describes the sculpture of a freshly unearthed Greek pediment: 'Flesh, reddish in tone; globe of eyes yellow, iris green, with a hole in the centre filled with black; black outlines to eyebrows and eyelids; hair and beard bright blue at the time of excavation, which disintegrated later into a greenish tone; circle of brown around the nipples.'

It should be mentioned at this point that, to the ancients, sculpture and painting were not conceived as isolated forms of art, i.e. as *objets d'art*, but as architectural elaboration. The fact that their sculpture attracted pigmentation underlined a concept of architecture as a polychromatic work of art. The Parthenon, for example, did not exist for its contemporaries as the pristine marble temple we see today, for, in 432 B.C., its internal and external friezes had been gilded and painted in contrasting hues above whitewashed columns (**1.1**).

While the idea of multicoloured temples was not at first readily accepted, the early nineteenth century saw new research into the colours of the past and into non-Western cultures. By 1829 J. I. Hittorff had published lithographic colour reconstructions, while Owen Jones in 1856—using the same medium—publicized the sumptuous hues of Byzantine and Moorish glazed tiles. His reconstructions of Egyptian, Persian, Venetian and Oriental coloration were offered to his Victorian counterparts as models for the embellishment of their adventure into a Revivalist architecture (**1.2**). There was now enough fuel to fire the imaginations of those designers who had begun to question the role of colour in architecture (a question, indeed, still posed and the central issue of this book).

While some followed Owen Jones' evangelical promotion of a coloured architecture, others fell under the spell of John Ruskin, who had spurned a skin-deep decoration in preference to the integrity of self-coloured materials. However, both approaches opened up a debate on environmental colour in which points were to be made by each camp. In his role of colour consultant to Paxton's Crystal Palace, Jones had prescribed red, blue and yellow paint for its interior and blue and white for its exterior, later proclaiming in his *The Grammar of Ornament* that it was only the highpoints in art which were epitomized by brilliant primary colours, decadent periods being synony-

1.1 (preceding page) Keble College, Oxford. Built between 1867 and 1883, William Butterfield's design for this university building (seen from its recent extension) attempted to create a truly constructional polychromy by employing the natural colours of stone and brickwork. PHOTO: ALAN COLEMAN (IVOR FIELDS PHOTOGRAPHIC)

1.2 Parthenon frieze (the Elgin Marbles). A reconstruction of the original colours of the metopes and triglyphs by the Royal Ontario Museum, Toronto. COURTESY: ROYAL ONTARIO MUSEUM

1.3 Lithographic plate from *The Grammar of Ornament*, Owen Jones, 1856. Jones was an architect and ornamental designer who compiled this sumptuous decorator's pattern book as a beacon in his quest for 'a new architectural style' in Victorian England.

1.3

mous with secondary and tertiary colours. Meanwhile, William Butterfield experimented with a patterned architecture exploiting self-coloured materials. He used glazed brickwork and natural stone on the All Saints' Church for the Ecclesiastical Society in London and exploited the inherent colours of brick on Oxford's Balliol Chapel and Keble College (**1.3**). Nevertheless, during these experiments with applied and intrinsic polychromy, the realization that the ancients had used brilliant colours continued to meet a lingering scepticism. As late as 1863—twelve years after the Great Exhibition—Sir Lawrence Alma-Tadema triggered a minor scandal with the unveiling of his painting *Phideas and the Painting of the Frieze of the Parthenon* (**1.4**). The fact that he had portrayed realistically its co-designer in the process of applying the paint was to cause a storm—incensing the sculptor Auguste Rodin to strike his breast exclaiming: 'I believe it here that these were never coloured.' Beyond the scepticism, however, a question arises concerning the function of this external decoration because, by comparison with the wider availability of colours in modern paints and their improved weathering properties, Phideas had worked from a limited palette of inferior pigment. One fact is certain: the colours were not applied as a protective barrier against the elements, as it was their lack of durability, without regular redecoration, which hastened the loss of so much of Phideas' work.

The portrait painter Sir William Beechey (1753–1839) offers one clue as to their significance. He observed that the lost colours were not simply a capricious decoration but appeared to respond to an established code of practice which assigned individual hues to specific components of a building. The archaeologist Frederick Poulson (1876–1950) developed this observation when remarking on the striking similarity between the richly painted treatments of reliefs on the Acquinetum pediment and the metopes of the Sicyonian Treasury. Helmets and clothes were blue and red respectively but each edged with a line of the other colour; whenever two or more articles of clothing or armour were worn, these were counter-changed. Similarly, the borders of overlapping shields signalled an alternation of red and blue. The tails and manes of horses and lions were also in red, but when several were superimposed blue was used to alternate the colour scheme.

A picture rapidly emerges of a colour system which deployed contrast as a means of visual emphasis and clarification. This seems entirely logical when, on the one hand, we consider that much of the elaboration was elevated high above eye level and, on the other, that the Greeks were masters of the optical illusion—a skill which their use of entasis (the subtle curving of architectural forms to correct perceptual distortion and reduce apparent weight) clearly demonstrates. The polychromatic extension of a three-dimensional experience, therefore, seems to have existed in classical Greek architecture as a

1.4 *Phideas and the Painting of the Frieze of the Parthenon*, Sir Lawrence Alma-Tadema, 1863. Depicting the ancient Greek love of primary colours on their buildings, this Victorian oil painting caused an uproar when it was first exhibited. COURTESY: BIRMINGHAM CITY MUSEUMS AND ART GALLERY

device to intensify form. It is found in the use of blue to underline the shadows on limewashed Ionian capitals; a use of two blues on the corrugations of triglyphs—a lighter on the face, and a darker on the indented facet—to accentuate their shape. It is also demonstrated in the red columns of Knossos, i.e. a use of an optically 'heavy' colour to emphasize the weight borne by supports, but perceived against the contrasting blue of their painted capitals and, indeed, of the Aegean Sea and sky (**1.5**).

If we take a second look at the colours of ancient Greece, we find another more deep-rooted function, for the pediments and friezes acted as gigantic billboards narrating the mythology of a Golden Age. Here, a strong colour—much as it does on modern hoardings—played a symbolic role. Blue, for example, was associated with 'truth' and 'integrity', colour attributes which were later to re-emerge in the cloaked Madonna of Christian symbolism. White was the basic colour of the Parthenon and of Athena's statue. The meaning of the Greek word 'parthenon' is synonymous with 'virginity', and white is still defiantly displayed by blushing Western brides. Red was ascribed to 'love' and 'sacrifice', the latter accounting for Dionysius' red face during the period of the annual wine festival; and, again, it is the colour which for psychological rather than mystical reasons finds its way into

1.5 Palace of Minos columns, Knossos, Crete. Red pigment reappeared on the columns at Knossos as a result of Sir Arthur Evans' restoration in 1926. The selection of pigments with a dark value such as red, ochre and black was an excellent Minoan design decision as they appear 'heavy' colours. PHOTO: WILLIAM TAYLOR

modern bar interiors. Other Greek gods were also vested in their appropriate colours—some being painted different hues to reflect the changing cycle of seasons. However, the reddening process is at the very root of symbolism and to learn more we must retrace our steps back through time before even the first builders and into the caves of prehistoric man.

It was here in a primeval society that colour was seen to embody a magical power capable of influencing events; the daubing of a corpse with red ochre, for instance, could prepare the deceased for a life beyond the grave. This use of red is practically universal throughout the diverse structures of colour symbolism in both ancient and primeval societies. It is still evident today among primitive tribes, when the facial pallor of the departed is 'enlivened' with a touch of rouge. (Indeed I remember the corpse of my own grandfather being decorated in this way.) Apart from its widespread availability as a pigment, red is a hue common to all races as the life-giving colour of blood. It is the colour of passion; a colour to be summoned from within to the surface of the skin in order to convey emotion via the blush of love or the flush of anger. It is also the colour to be artificially applied to the exterior surface of the skin as, in the case of warpaint, a kind of heraldic anger intensifying and prolonging the heat of the moment or, in the case of lipstick and face powder, a form of 'warpaint' intended to attract or rejuvenate. The facial reddening of the living, the dead, and the inanimate was practised in ancient Egypt where extremes in complexion were highly prized. In order to enhance the redness of their own pigmentation, the Egyptians used body cosmetics, and red was also applied to the faces of their mummies, and to that of the Sphinx. Red paint, in one form or another, has been used as a symbol of man's aspiration to a continued existence on most of the paraphernalia of his physical and spiritual kit—from the fertility icons and wall paintings of prehistoric men to the exterior façades of medieval cathedrals. Modern society continues to imbue some colours with meaning and a common connotation of red is that of impending danger. This association is reflected in the traffic signal—a colour warning which may have distant roots in the prehistoric day–night cycle, when a red dusk signalled the end of the active phase and the need to withdraw from the perils of the black night into the safety of caves.

Among the first builders there existed no real difference between construction and image-making as far as usefulness was concerned. Their initial makeshift dwellings and nomadic shelters functioned simply to protect them from the elements. Coloured images—spontaneously redirected from cave to built form—continued to protect them from the spiritual powers which were felt to be as real as the forces of nature. It is interesting to note that this basic function of colour occurs in almost all primitive and ancient cultures of the world, and that always the same type of strong, saturated hues were used: notably red, blue, yellow, green, black and white, together with the precious metals—gold and silver. A factor which confuses any detailed comparison of symbolism among cultures, however, is that colour can be used to signify so many different concepts, and that these concepts are dependent upon the structure of a given society. The uses of symbolic colour mainly functioned in areas such as religion, mythology and astrology, ceremonial ritual, for healing purposes, and to denote status, race, the elements of science and points of the compass.

If one could journey through time around the sites of the world's earliest buildings and cities, a kaleidoscope of colourful architecture would be encountered. For instance, the layered fortifications of ziggurats in Mesopotamia—a civilization dominated by the study of astrology—were, according to Leonard Woolley, each coloured in hues assigned to the planets of the solar system. The ziggurat at Ur (now in modern Iraq) is among the oldest structures, and descriptions of the colours of its four concentric walls, successively black, red, and topped with blue and gold, conjure images of a gigantic and brilliant helter-skelter. Similarly Herodotus' description of the city of Ectabana, built in the fourth century B.C., is of a layered construction, coloured white at its base through stages of black, red, blue and orange to gold and silver at its pinnacle. Similar to the stratified coloration of ziggurats in Asia Minor was the colouring of the pyramids, temples and shrines of Inca, Mayan and Toltec cultures of Central and South America. The walls of the ancient Chinese capital of Peking were painted in red and roofs within the city coloured yellow. Red and yellow symbolized positive–negative and were also associated with good and evil spirits—the yellow roofs acting to camouflage inhabitants from any evil spirits who happened to pass overhead. The ancient Egyptians actually idolized colour and assigned hues to the sculptured manifestations of a deity system which, as did earlier religions, centred on the worship of the sun. They also employed a positive paint application on their buildings. This involved a skill which accentuated architectural detail in a climate where plastic form, if softly modelled, would appear diffuse. The interiors of their temples often contained blue painted ceilings to symbolize the heavens (a colour use later found on the vaulted ceilings of Gothic churches) above green floors to represent the meadows of the Nile.

The Greeks, as previously mentioned, loved to cover their buildings with colour washes; their deep interest in its potential initiated the first serious study of colour principles by Pythagoras and Aristotle. The discovery of Pompeii and Herculaneum almost intact beneath Vesuvius' ash in the early eighteenth century unearthed a new degree of brilliance in colours which was to change forever our picture of Roman architecture. In discussing the Roman importation of the Greek pigments, Pliny describes the colour-making compounds first in terms of their healing properties, for their sources were the same as those of medicinal potions.

As knowledge of pigments increased, architectural colour became richer. Also, the introduction of egg and oil binders, together with the invention of fresco (the addition of pigment to damp plaster) increased their permanence. Advances in the processes of pottery glazing and glass-making combined to help further extend the designer's colour range, and to introduce a new and scintillating medium. It was glass that gave colour a luminosity which was to be so beautifully exploited in Greek, Roman and Byzantine mosaics and later in the stained-glass windows of medieval cathedrals. Rich colour was an intrinsic element of glass-making because, until the Renaissance, clear glass was much more difficult to achieve. A multicoloured sunlight, therefore, poured into medieval cathedrals but it also illuminated the brightly painted surfaces of their interiors—a colour experience which was matched and, according to James Ward, often overshadowed by a corresponding application of pigment and gilding to external façades. Traces of medieval colours are still distinguishable on the exteriors of many French cathedrals, such as the flecks of red, blue and green at Angers, and the red stain on Notre Dame. There is also strong evidence of similar decoration used in England during the Middle Ages. For example, when discussing the great west front of Wells Cathedral in *Gothic Architecture*, Cecil Stewart states: '. . . its one hundred and seventy six full-length statues were brilliantly coloured. The niches were dark red, and the figures and drapery were painted in yellow ochre, with eyes and hair picked out in black and the lips in red. In the central group of the Virgin and Child, the Virgin's robe was black with a green lining, while the Child's robe was crimson, the composition being set on a background of

1.6 Merry-go-Round, St. Giles Fair, Oxford. The gilt and 'garish' colours of traditional fairground decoration have roots which go back beyond their medieval associations. PHOTO: ALAN COLEMAN (IVOR FIELDS PHOTOGRAPHIC)

red and green diaper. There is evidence, from plugholes, that the statues were further enriched with gilded metal ornament. Above, the row of angels were painted rosy red.'

It was as an extension of an aspiring Gothic architecture that symbolic colour appeared on buildings for the last time. It was later to disappear under the Reformation scrubbing brush and the Puritan white-wash—instruments of a new brand of religious fervour which set out to rid religious buildings of their sensuous and pagan overtones.

However, some evidence of the lost colours occasionally flicker and dance in the modern setting, kept alive by the undercurrents of a folk art tradition, the ceremonies of pagan festivals and the symbolism of religious ritual. Morris dancers, for example, still carry the spring green of fertility around their maypole. The Pope remains cloaked in the precious purple of the ancients—a pigment so difficult to achieve that it was reserved by the Romans (and the Greeks before them) only for those of the highest rank. Although deprived of much of their original meaning some of the ancient reds, yellows, blues and greens escaped the puritanical purge by keeping on the move. They remain in currency with the bargee's art of longboat decoration. Also, they are still meticulously painted over the trappings of other portable environments such as the circus, gypsy caravans, and the travelling fairground. It is the sheer uninhibited exuberance of fairground paintwork and gilding which possibly represents a reasonable simulation of the coloration of an ancient Greek city (**1.6**). Its decoration comes close to reflecting the methods used by designers such as Phideas to extend, via polychromy, the experience of architectural and sculptural form. This three-dimensional employment of colour is also mirrored in the cave painter's art for, along the technicolor tunnels of Lascaux and Altamira, areas of coloured pigment not only described the shapes of animals but also responded to the shapes of natural projections and hollows in the cave wall.

A similar handling of colour can be found in an important turning point in the development of modern architecture which occurred in Holland during the 1920s. Primary colours on buildings reappeared, but this time as part of a de Stijl re-examination of their basic spatial effects and on an architecture stripped of ornamentation.

While Mondrian attempted to tame pure colours on canvas by containing them in grid-plan abstractions reminiscent of the criss-crossing of Dutch dykes, Gerrit Rietveld projected them as a means of spatial control on to the internal and external planes of his architecture. Through a use of red, blue and yellow, he 'fixed' the elevational modulations of the Schröder House in space. When necessary, he articulated the visual 'pushing' and 'pulling' qualities of colour to induce illusions of increased depth (**1.7**).

1.7 Schröder House, Utrecht, by Gerrit Rietveld, 1924. As opposed to the Constructivist use of colour to emphasize function, the Purists employed its advancing and receding qualities to define space. Piet Mondrian's paintings using only the primaries with black, white and grey deeply influenced the Dutch de Stijl architects such as J. J. P. Oud and Gerrit Rietveld.
COURTESY: RIETVELD ARCHIVE

During the birth pangs of the modern movement there had been philosophical clashes between another de Stijl exponent, Theo van Doesburg, and the French architect Le Corbusier. Despite their differences, both employed pulsating colours in their designs—the former carrying them into interiors as had Art Nouveau designers before him, but this time to define the hard edges of a modernist geometry rather than as a sensuous adjunct to the curve. Le Corbusier, on the other hand, loved the 'powerful hum of colour' especially as stabs of bright paintwork against the white of his façades. In his large-scale housing projects he used colour to emphasize the indented rhythms of external walls—employing paint to separate 'inside' from 'outside' in the transitional space of balconies and deep recesses (**1.8**).

By contrast to the more scientifically controlled colour schemes of the

1.8 *Unité d'Habitation*, Marseilles, by Le Corbusier, 1952–55. Typical of Le Corbusier's use of exterior colour is his insertion of primary hues into recesses and around apertures in the façade. In this way, a modified natural light, tinted by paint, is deflected into interior space. PHOTO: GRAHAM COOPER

modernists, remnants of more decorative colour can also be found on other twentieth-century 'shrines'—modern temples such as those by Wallis, Gilbert & Partners which, being designed for an Outer London of the late twenties and early thirties, were given a cocktail of Egyptian and American Red Indian inspired decoration and dedicated to the glory of Firestone and Hoover (**1.9**).

The epitome of them all, however, is that monumental shrine to contemporary art situated not too far from the once multicoloured cathedral of Notre Dame. It is the Pompidou Centre, which makes interesting comparisons with the Parthenon because in its original conception the west elevation was intended to double as an audio-visual screen system—a cinematic projection of architecture electronically updating the comic-strip format of the Elgin marbles. However, it is the existence of brilliant colours on the columns of ducting on the east elevation which has traceable connections with the colours of antiquity. In citing the brilliance of paintwork found on agricultural

1.9 Hoover building, Perivale, Middlesex. Designed by Wallis, Gilbert & Partners in 1932, this façade is held by many to represent the finest of the Art Deco style. One of its architects, Thomas Wallis, firmly believed that its colours would project a beneficial company image. He saw them as creating a sense of pride in the workforce and as a good advertisement of their product. PHOTO: ALAN COLEMAN (IVOR FIELD PHOTOGRAPHIC)

machinery as having direct influence on his colour choice, Richard Rogers indirectly heeds the High Victorian call to the colours by Owen Jones, and reinstates the ancient hues in an architecture of high technology (**1.10**).

Under the pressure of dogmatic Ruskinian views of what constituted 'bad taste', the Victorian excursion into architectural polychromy had been short-lived. Instead, the resurrected ancient colours appeared as embellishment to the metal of a machine age, and an eye-catching protective paintwork was applied to iron structures such as bridges, to the coachwork of steam engines, and to the working parts of industrial and agricultural machinery. It was this tradition which inspired Rogers over a century later and brought about a landmark in a return to outside colour as an architectural design tool.

1.10 Pompidou Centre, Paris. It is interesting to note that Piano and Rogers' coded colours on the rue de Renard elevation of their high-tech 'mechanism' may not be too dissimilar from the original colours of Notre Dame cathedral. Together with green, orange and ochre, traces of red pigment—possibly with 'hot gospel' rather than 'hot water' connotations—have been detected on the cathedral's façades. PHOTO: TOM PORTER

2 COLOUR ON THE WALL

After its beginnings in the late sixties wall painting has come through into the eighties with flying colours. There is, of course, some precedent for this particular phenomenon—the paint of Victorian wall advertisements, although faded, is still discernible on older city brickwork. Also, the monumental billboards whose hand-painted messages address the American car-oriented suburbs have enjoyed a fashionable vogue, and the first of the large murals which appeared in New York's inner city have been received favourably both by their immediate street audience and by environmental psychologists, who see them as important cultural and community landmarks. Wall painting has since flourished internationally as an activity involving individual artists, muralist groups and members of local neighbourhoods. The initial experiments concentrated on improving the visual lot of slum and ghetto dwellers but soon proliferated into as many forms as there are regional, social and ethnic differences.

There is no single movement directing this activity, and the functions of murals are as diverse as their settings. Some are painted in anger to protest against social and environmental deprivation, while others lovingly celebrate local history or heroes, or simply bring art into public view. Apart from the spontaneous walls of 'pride' and 'respect' painted by ethnic minority groups and the universal walls of discontent painted by phantom brigades of muralists, sponsorship is varied. In America, for instance, there are the museum-financed projects and syndication by such bodies as the Public Art Fund; in the U.K., regional arts associations and local authorities give healthy encouragement to those who wish to paint the town. Much of this activity, however, has been aimed at improving dilapidated environments, but in France a recent sponsor—in the form of local government—has commissioned artists to soften the impact of a new architecture (**2.1**).

There are also commercially sponsored murals such as the one by the doyen of wall painters, Les Grimes, who died in an accident in 1968 while completing ten years' work on his legendary *Hog's Heaven*. This painting functions as a hoarding, tracing the life of a pig from piglet to sausage around the exterior of a Los Angeles meat-processing plant. Another exists on the side wall of the Schmitt Music Centre in Minneapolis: it portrays a vast expanse of sheet music drawn from Ravel's 'Gaspard de la Nuit'. At a cost of $12,000, it took ten days to brick up thirty-two windows, prepare the surface and apply the paint (**2.2**). An interesting footnote was a resulting action by the American holders of Ravel's copyright to sue for over-exposure of his music. The threat was scotched, however, by the muralist's inclusion of several 'mistakes'—a lucky foresight which, according to Schmitt's Publicity Officer, meant that the whole affair ended on a 'happy note'.

In total contrast are the community-based murals which depict events and characters indigenous to their setting. *The Good, the Bad, and the Ugly* (better known as 'Morgan's Wall') was situated in Battersea, London, and recognised as a classic of its genre. Sixty helpers working under the direction of artist Brian Barnes graphically documented local discontent at the decline of

2.1 (preceding page) Wall painting by Bernard Lassus, Uckange, France. One of the aims of artist Bernard Lassus is to underline the distinction between 'tactile' and 'visual' scales of vision; in other words, the perceptual divergence between the starkness of constructed form and the rich variety of form that the eye seeks. PHOTO: BERNARD LASSUS

2.2

2.2 *Gaspard de la Nuit*, Minneapolis. This painted expanse of sheet music magnifies the third section of the 'Scarbo' movement of Ravel's 'Gaspard de la Nuit', composed in 1908. Here, the wall acts as backdrop to yet another publicity stunt—an outdoor performance by American virtuoso Van Cliburn. COURTESY: SCHMITT MUSIC CENTRE

2.3 Community mural at Wandsworth, London. This wall painting, funded by the Arts Council of Great Britain, was designed and executed over a twelve-month period by the residents of two nearby housing estates under the direction of artist Brian Barnes. It celebrates their memorable day-trip to Southend and accurately portrays sixty-four locals together with a Donald McGill cartoon character culled from a picture postcard. The excursion was specifically arranged for the purpose of taking photographs of individuals for incorporation in the design—a decision taken at a public meeting held prior to the trip. Another decision was to overstate the colours of its emulsion paint in order to counteract the fading effects of ultra-violet light. PHOTO: ALAN COLEMAN (IVOR FIELDS PHOTOGRAPHIC)

their area along its 200 ft. length—incidents being spontaneously recorded as they happened over the two years of its execution. In an angry preservationist campaign during which, at its height, the artist was arrested, the wall finally fell in 1979 before the bulldozers of 'progress'. A more recent community mural carried out under the guidance of Brian Barnes celebrates a day coach trip to the seaside by fifty residents in the Wandsworth area of London (**2.3**).

Wall art has become an intrinsic part of the urban experience, with places as far apart as Swindon and Cincinnati, Manchester and Manhattan containing a wealth of well-documented murals. Its newfound status is expressed, for instance, in the meticulous restoration of some faded walls in New York, in commissions emanating from such august bodies as the Senate of Berlin, and in attracting artists of the calibre of Eduardo Paolozzi and Victor Vasarely. There is also the challenge of scale and in playing its extremes. The leading American artist Gene Davis takes more than just casual notice of environmental context. His micro-paintings—diminutive postage stamps of flat colour strategically positioned within rooms to punctuate key spatial points—miniaturize the concept of gallery art to Lilliputian proportions, reminding one of the minute colour chips used by psychologists to elicit responses (**2.4**). At the other end of the scale his gargantuan street paintings transform outdoor floorscape into vibrant fields of delineated colour. At the same time they introduce a scale which questions the way in which we view a work of art. *Franklin's Footpath*—a mammoth work executed in emulsion paint on the tarmacadam of the parkway approach to Philadelphia's Museum of Modern Art—covered 38,000 square feet. It captivated that city for five years before its erosion due to constant usage and weathering. *Artpark* is another even bigger work on the concrete surface of an active carpark in Niagara, New York. In consuming 540 gallons of water-based paint, it claims to be the largest painting in the world (Guinness Book of Records, 1979) (**2.5**).

Another floorscape project is the amusing installation at Evry new town in France by Gerard Singer. This employed an ink blue polyester medium which, seemingly from an overturned tin of paint, floods across a children's playground and empties into a courtyard lake amidst the muted colours of surrounding housing (**2.6**).

This attraction to the floor plane seems a natural extension of façade painting in which muralists concentrated on the same dreary walls which had previously caught the reproachful eye of the moonlighting graffitist. However, an almost universal claim by European and American muralists that their painted walls escape defacement by aerosol led the author—together with a group of first-year architecture students—to conduct an experiment in a little-used graffiti-ridden pedestrian underpass in Heading-

2.4 Micro-painting, Gene Davis. The essential ratio between actual size and apparent size is recreated in the diminutive end of Davis' preoccupation with scale in painting.

2.5 *Artpark*, Gene Davis. Davis puts the finishing touches to his mammoth acrylic floor-painting in the carpark of Niagara, New York. Its sheer size is important, not only because—like his micro-paintings—it compels an awareness of self, but it also questions our approach to works of art. Instead of viewing a painting head-on, surrounded by a frame and the white walls of a gallery, we can look down from a helicopter, walk or dance over it, or actually park cars on it.

2.6 Blue floorscape, Evry, France. This landscape in polyester was conceived by sculptor Gerard Singer to entertain the children of 'nouveau ville' housing designed by Emile Aillaud. Many such environmental projects, designed with children in mind, have been initiated by the new breed of 'town artists', often working in conjunction with architects or residents' associations in the Scottish and English new towns. PHOTO: GERARD SINGER

2.7 Pedestrian underpass, Headington, Oxford. A first-year architectural design project for an urban space by Katrine Brustad, Oxford Polytechnic. Her idea—sponsored by the City of Oxford Highways Committee—was based on three assumptions. First, that its colours would attract a greater usage for the subway; on entering pedestrians would be provided with a rapidly changing chromatic stimulus. Second, that its four emulsion paint hues would, via colour interaction, provide a wider chromatic experience. Third, that its vertical bands might function as 'blackboards' to contain any subsequent graffiti and thereby ease maintenance. Local shopowners, familiar with its previous abuse, were pessimistic but two years of freedom from the aerosol followed its installation. PHOTO: TOM PORTER

ton, Oxford. Sponsored by a sympathetic City Council and an understanding local firm of painters and decorators, the aim of the project was twofold: to see if the installation of cheerful hues on the drab walls might reduce vandalism; and to discover if a positive colour would attract more pedestrians to use the tunnel rather than traverse the busy London Road above. Discreet 'before' and 'after' observations (the latter occurring beyond the 'novelty period' immediately after redecoration) determined comparative levels of usage, and regular checks were made over an ensuing two-year period to record any subsequent defacement. The first part of the test proved disappointing—only a slight increase in pedestrians taking the longer, although safer and now more colourful route through the underpass. However, total success was claimed by the complete absence of graffiti despite the project's media exposure and its intermittent use by fans of visiting football teams (**2.7**).

The resurgence of wall painting derives from an age-old tradition. The use of architecture as a support on which to hang a narrative or an abstract paintwork did not begin in New York in the 1960s or with the Mexican murals of Rivera, Orozco and Siquieros in the 1920s; it is a practice as ancient as

2.8 *Trompe l'oeil* wall decoration, Recco, Italy. An illusory reality of windows, shutters, stonework and other façade embellishments is extremely important in traditional Italian architecture. It represents an architecture often non-existent, with pigment providing a brush-applied status which the occupier can communicate to others. PHOTO: RICCARDO ZANETTA

building itself. In Central Europe the art survived from the Middle Ages, with splendid examples to be found in towns close to the German–Austrian border like Mittelwald and Oberammergau, on the painted churches of northern Romania and in many Italian cities. For example, at a time when the work of a skilled painter and decorator cost far less than the materials of rich ornamentation, the thrifty Genoese resorted to a sham decoration in order to bring an impression of opulence and elegance into their streets. Up until fifty years ago (although the local tradition seems to be reviving) a *trompe l'oeil* form of housepainting was an intensely serious preoccupation. This involved the skilful representation of cornices, rusticated stonework, stucco, windows—with shutters either open or closed—to fake a painted wealth of architectural detail otherwise lacking in their façades. By mixing illusion with reality, wall painting replaced the anonymity of existing buildings with an idealised version which clearly communicated the aspirations of their inhabitants (**2.8**).

It is not surprising that many similar examples of illusion-making appear within revivalist works as it is a skill at the very essence of fine art. Fabio Rieti is the author of a Super-Realist mural depicting eight apartment windows which, set among their real counterparts, look from rue Quincampoix into Place Beaubourg in Paris with a realism so convincing that their presence goes almost entirely undetected (**2.9**). The *Wall of Windows* in the Manhattan warehouse district of SoHo also enlists a Super-Realist technique, this time to mirror in illusory paintwork the existing reality of one windowed façade on the blank face of another (**2.10**). Although painstakingly applied for different reasons—in this case to draw attention to the sad decline in the city's cast iron heritage—such murals take us closer to a use of colour in the environment which responds directly to its architectural context.

2.9 Super-realist window, rue Quincampoix, Paris. One of eight false windows painted by Fabio Rieti to disguise an airduct built on to the end of a row of apartments facing Place Beaubourg. By using paint to mimic fenestration, Rieti melts the intrusion of a concrete mass into the total impression of the street façade.

A further example exists on the Laycock Primary School in Islington, London. Here designs produced by schoolchildren under the direction of David Cashman and Roger Fagin display a profound regard for the quality of surface—a not unfamiliar form of façade decoration which shows how paint can radically alter an austere architectural character (**2.11**). Generally, the instrument of colour can be used to invest existing buildings with all the elements of expression, story-telling, ambiguity and communication that it lost some time ago. The more recent return to façade elaboration by artists has, at least, familiarized the contemporary designer and his public with a wider experience—albeit on a single plane—of exterior colour denied him by the restraint of the International Style.

Given the fact that the more recent trend in wall painting has been the conscious extension by artists of architecture, the odd thing is that what began as playful decoration is now seriously influencing architecture itself.

2.10 *Wall of Windows,* New York, Richard Haas. This acrylic wall painting represents a conservationist form of protest as it was devised to protect the future of its support—a cast iron warehouse building in the SoHo district of Manhattan. Its illusory windows—all but two meticulously handpainted in the Super-Realist manner to mirror the fenestration of its other street façade—have attempted successfully to draw attention to the fine quality of cast iron detailing in an area where their melting pot value as scrap has encouraged ruthless demolition.
PHOTO: TOM PORTER

2.11 Laycock Primary School childrens' mural, Islington, London. Each of the School's pupils was asked to design a coloured panel on a template screenprinted to represent a grid of brickwork to a small scale. From over three hundred designs, sixteen were selected for rescaling on to two large, blank street façades of which this is one. The abstract frames were designed by David Cashman and Roger Fagin who co-ordinated the entire project. PHOTO: GRAHAM NASH

2.11

8916 HF 78

The flatness and implied inviolability of a wall is being questioned by architects. Post-Modernist buildings, for example, are filled with illusion, with some designed to incorporate symbolic graphics on a façade scale.

There is also another development: the emergence of a new breed of designer. He is a muralist—an artist who concentrates on the application of colour to a complete architectural scheme rather than to a single wall. This development has shifted a colour decision inside and alongside the architect's whole design process. This new approach is epitomized in the work of industrial artist Yehiel Rabinowitz. After serving an apprenticeship to urban scale by executing many large Parisian wall paintings—including his formidable mural on the Montsouris Telephone Exchange (**2.12**)—Rabinowitz has devoted his talents to the creation of large thematic designs. These bring images of the countryside to the walls of industrial workshops such as those at Douvrin and the Grand-Couronne Regie Renault plants. As part of his conception of industrial aesthetics, Rabinowitz's designs range from unabashed exterior decoration to the more architecturally reverent. He claims, above all, that colour—rather than introducing artificial atmospheres—should give 'life' to the existing features of a building.

The work of the colourists has drawn attention to some of the important contributions that colour can make to the outside environment, and these are the subject of the next chapter.

2.12 Wall painting, Montsouris Telephone Exchange, Paris. This mural is an example of a recurring theme in the urban work of Yehiel Rabinowitz, an 'industrial decorator' who imports abstracted rural images and colours into the heart of the city and into industrial workshops. PHOTO: YEHIEL RABINOWITZ

500

3 THE USE OF ENVIRONMENTAL COLOUR

The colour of a city is an aspect of its history. Until the early nineteenth century, European towns and cities developed by a slow process of organic growth, generally employing materials indigenous to their regions. Architectural styles evolved within the limitations of available materials and this disciplined the form of the buildings, which were related to human scale. The constant use of local materials produced urban settings with visual harmony despite a diversity of forms. An example of this is Oxford's High Street. Here, buildings reflect several hundred years of stylistic change, but all are unified by scale, material and, especially, by colour. Colour in Oxford responds to the warmth of local sandstone and is deployed with apparent co-ordination. The predominant ochres (now replaced by synthetic equivalents) had originally only to be transported from Shotover Hill at the city's edge—a famous source of highly prized yellow ochre.

Outside the conurbations, the colours of agricultural buildings were either blended with or perceptually 'detached' from the colour of their landscape settings. Where an ochre was used it would be the same as the earth upon which the farm building stood—offering a camouflaged security. Where farms were whitewashed, the resulting contrast identified the farmer's place of refuge from a distance. Generally, the colour decision was disciplined simply by the cheapness of applying local deposits of coloured earth or using them to tint or stain distemper and limewash. In turn, this process created architectural 'colour maps' in which certain colours became identified with particular regions. In a rural British Isles, for example, the national palette contained pinks and reds in the east and west, with umbers to the north and south surrounding a hinterland of yellow ochre.

Meanwhile, back in the towns and cities where architecture creates its own backdrop, there was always access to the deposits of local earth pigments for painting stucco façades. For those who could afford the protection of oil-based paints for exposed woodwork and the status of 'foreign' colours, there was the diversity of imported pigments. Today the designer can select colours for external use from an assortment of similarly priced and reasonably stable paint colours, but this was not the case in the past when pigments varied wildly both in cost and quality. For example, in the early nineteenth century the association of the brighter colours with wealth stemmed from the fact that blues, organic yellows and reds and some greens were ten times, and often one hundred times, the price of the common earth pigments.

It is through such limitations of selection that the architecture of cities and regions all over the world has come to be associated traditionally with particular ranges of colour. For instance, the ochres and reds of Lyons; and, among the blues and reds, the predominance of a 'Maria Theresa' yellow in central Vienna—its eighteenth-century plasterwork now being restored in stupendous streets like the Heiligenkreuzer Hof. There are also the brickdust reds and Georgian greens of a revamped Savannah, the pinks of Suffolk and Devon cottages, and the brilliant reds, blues and yellows of houses on the Adriatic island of Burano (**3.1**).

In order to protect colour traditions certain cities—such as Venice—exercise legislative control. Its citizens are restrained from painting façades in anything but the prescribed range of earth pigments comprising ochre, umber, sienna and red. In other places with a colour-conscious heritage in Europe as well as in towns in New England like Salem, Mass., advisory groups of historians and designers have together researched the specific colours used historically. These projects, on an urban scale, replicate the meticulous detective work of restorers such as those who painstakingly returned Le Corbusier's interior colours for Villa Savoy—dilapidated by wartime occupation—to their original state.

The chromatic identity of certain structures is immutable; no one today, for instance, is likely to gold-leaf the red oxide of San Francisco's Golden Gate Bridge (although gold was its originally intended colour). Similarly, the idea of redecorating the White House in vermilion or, conversely, whitewashing the brickwork of William Morris's 'Red House' is unthinkable. Nevertheless, something very like this has been done to urban environments; in Turin, for instance, which perhaps can boast the only example of environmental colour planned on an urban scale.

Environmental colour on a city scale: Turin

In 1800, a Council of Builders was set up to develop and apply a colour plan for the entire city—a project which was to establish environmental standards with surprisingly sophisticated specifications. Their concept was to invest

3.1 (preceding page) A marvellous island of colour at Burano, near Venice. Its harmonious orchestration has occurred without any masterplanning except that of an individual instinct within a collective consciousness tempered by tradition. PHOTO: PIETRO FONTANA

3.2 Turin colour map. A schematic map computer-generated by Colorterminal Ivi, Milan, showing the early-nineteenth-century parent colours for processional routes leading to Turin's Piazza Castello. Contrary to the popular notion that this city was exclusively coated in a 'Turin yellow', a predominance of ochre was originally used to 'frame' and 'background' a contrast with a co-ordinated variety of secondary colours. The colour samples below the map illustrate the detective work of Giovanni Brino and his team in identifying the most popular paints used between 1800 and 1850 from documents in the City Archive. They are ordered in terms of importance and annotated according to Munsell specification. COURTESY: GIOVANNI BRINO

principal streets and squares characterized by a uniform architecture with colours according to a co-ordinated system. Based on the checking of applications for the redecoration of buildings, the Council devised a series of chromatic pathways founded upon popular city colours—coloured routes which followed the major processional approaches to Turin's ideal centre—the Piazza Castello (**3.2**). The major routes were interconnected by a network of smaller streets and squares for which secondary and more variegated

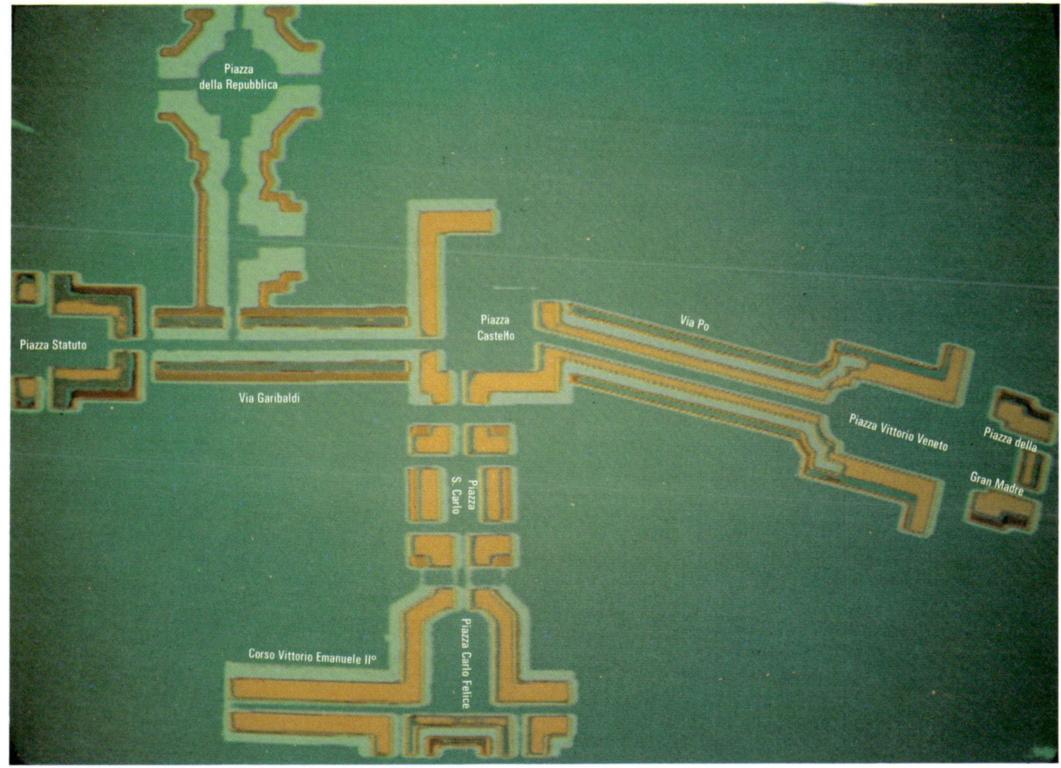

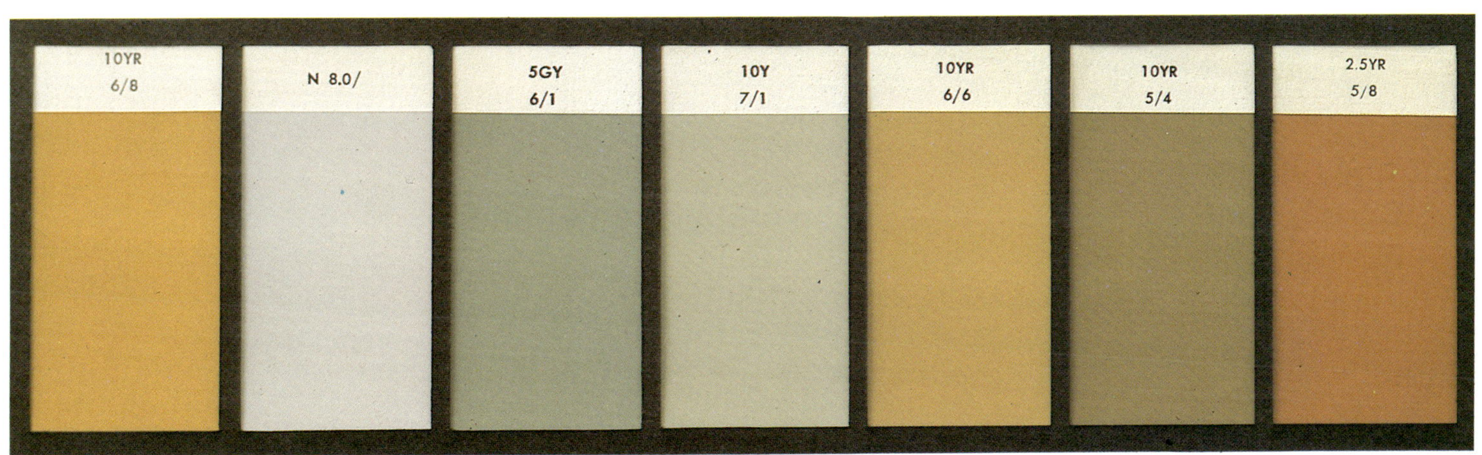

.2

colour sequences were prescribed. The basic scheme enlisted around eighty different colours, which were deployed to form a continuous and, at the same time, changing progression of experience.

After surviving a series of bureaucratic changes, the Council was abolished in 1845. No one knows just how long the original colour scheme survived, but it existed as one of Turin's distinguishing features, praised by such illustrious visitors as Friedrich Nietzsche in the late nineteenth century and Henry James in the early twentieth century.

By complete contrast to the breadth of the Council's colour range, the image of this city in recent decades has changed to one of monochrome. This is due to a pervading 'Turin yellow' which, because of indiscriminate redecoration together with a misconception that it is a colour traditionally associated with its architecture, blankets the city. This yellow not only covers all kinds of buildings but in one undifferentiating colour it also blurs the distinction among their materials, structure and the variety of space they define.

In December 1978 a restoration programme was set up by Enzo Biffi Gentili, the Municipality's Supervisor of Housing. The project is now conducted by a team which includes architects Germano Tagliasacehi and Riccardo Zanetta, historical advisor Franco Rosso, colourist Jorrit Tornquist and Romano Guietti (Colorterminal Ivi), under the direction of architect Giovanni Brino. The reconstruction and publication of the nineteenth-century colour map by reference to the well-documented archives and surviving paint samples, and its Munsell annotation, are already accomplished. The application of these colours to the original city centre and their extension to the area occupied by modern Turin is gathering momentum. Already over one thousand redecorated buildings have been incorporated into the revised colour system. The team, armed with the evidence of an historical masterplan, evaluate requests for repainting in consultation with owners and painters and decorators (**3.3**).

A sympathetic supporter of the Turin experiment is architect Paolo Portoghesi—himself a masterly colourist. However, he suggests that the danger in restoration (whether of a building to its 'original' state, or the reconstruction of urban polychromy) is that it might freeze a single phase of an evolving culture. Such reconstructions should, by taking account of change in popular taste, avoid the trap of wiping out any opportunity for reinterpretation. In order to illustrate his point, Portoghesi cites two very different colour conceptions of the 'ancient' centre of Rome. Its modern impression is determined by the widespread use of ochre compared with the popular fashion for a silvery graffito work which actually proliferated during the Renaissance. This is still concealed beneath layers of differing pigments—each reflecting the changing tastes of time.

3.3 a, b and c Turin colour restorations. The restoration of Turin's original masterplan for colour is accomplished at the rate of around one thousand buildings a year by the persuasive powers of Giovanni Brino and his design team during the evaluation of annual requests for repainting historic buildings. COURTESY: GIOVANNI BRINO

SERVIZI D'IGIENE E SANITA

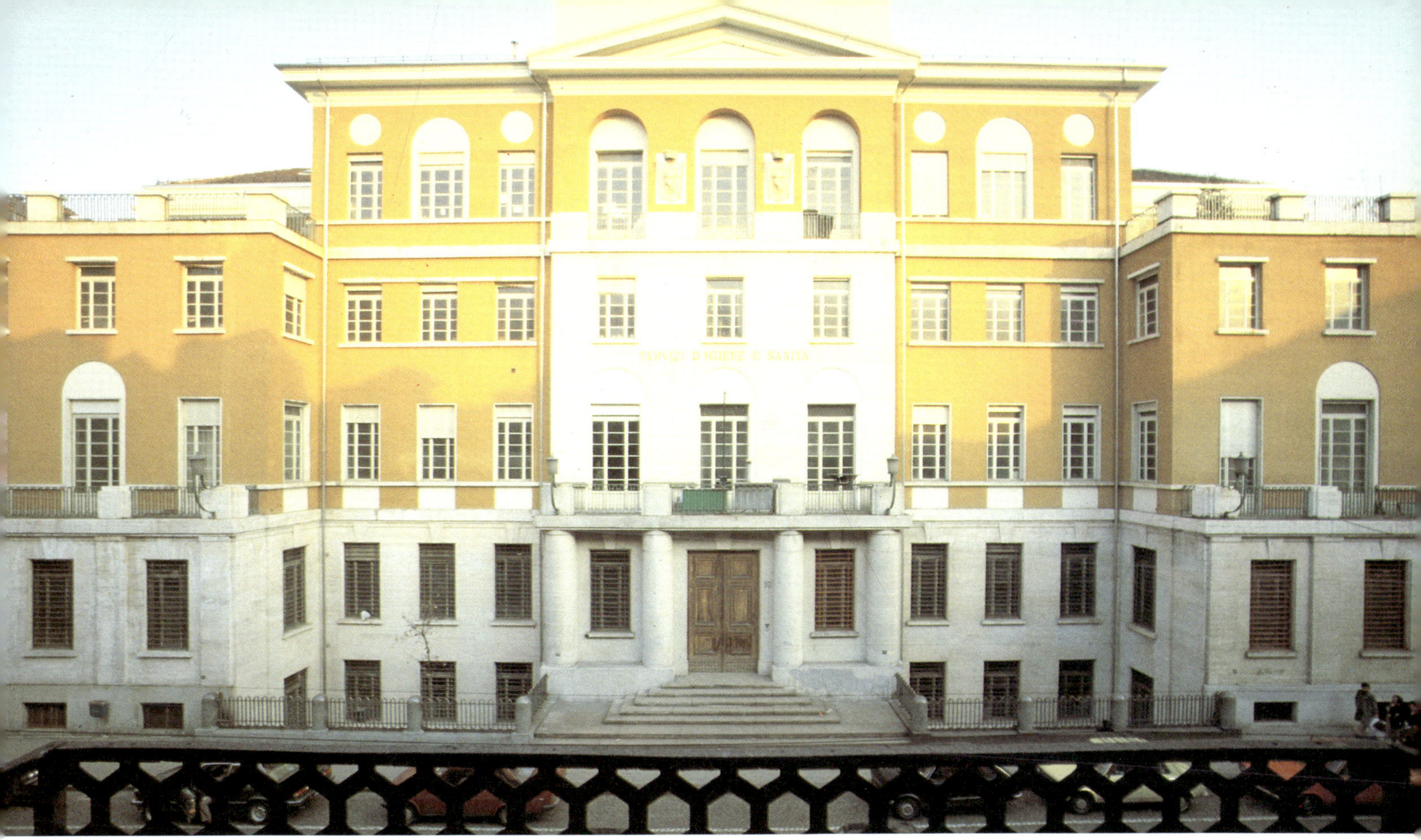

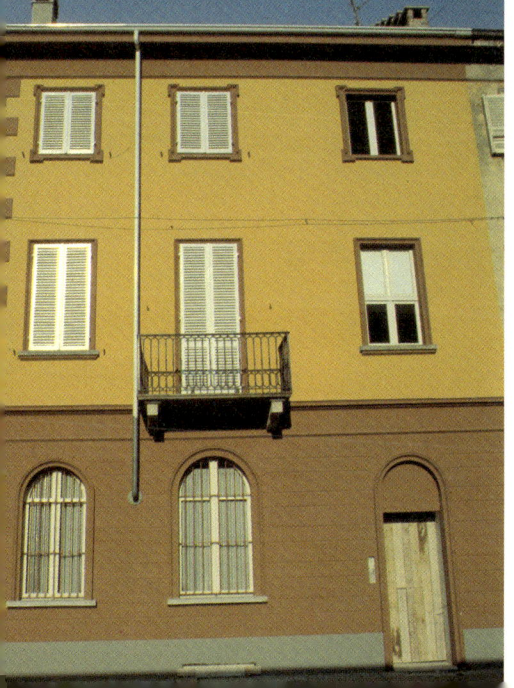

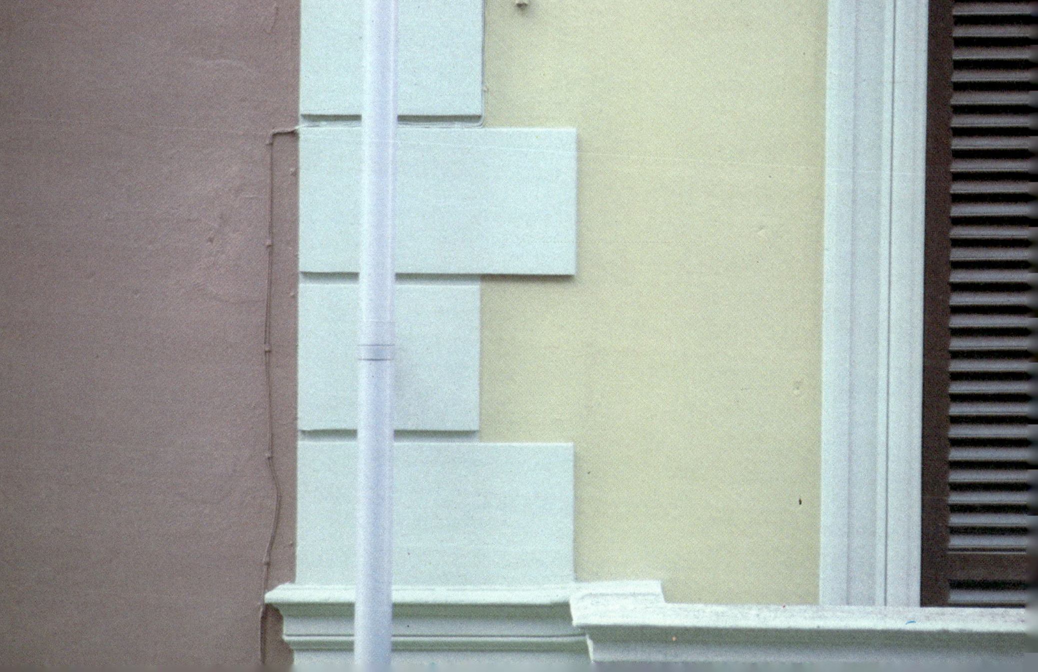

Environmental colour in France: Jean-Philippe Lenclos

An updated version of the research carried out by Turin's Council of Builders is found in France where, alongside the erection of new towns, an attempt is being made to develop a co-ordinated palette for application to modern architecture. A leading figure in this movement is Jean-Philippe Lenclos, a designer who, in order to preserve a sense of place in the face of the spreading anonymity of concrete, has turned to the study of colours traditionally applied to buildings. In essence, Lenclos has devised an exciting and comprehensive analysis which aims to codify the language of environmental colour. His investigation is both simple and objective in its classification of architectural and natural colour across France—a country with a diversity of region, climate and architecture.

Phase one of Lenclos' analysis involves the collection of colour samples directly from selected sites within each region. Fragments of paint and

3.4 Part of Lenclos' colour study of Toulouse, France. After the collection of actual samples from the architectural and natural colours within a selected site area, Jean-Philippe Lenclos and his team paint faithfully colour-matched renderings under the controlled light of the studio. These are then assembled into colour charts—'chromatic alphabets'—from which a vocabulary of appropriate colours can be prescribed for re-application to both new and existing buildings in the region. As a result of his extensive research, Lenclos has produced a user's guide for French designers (*Selecteur d'Harmonies*) so that their architectural colour prescriptions can identify with existing environments. PHOTO: R. MEYER

3.5 Colour analysis, Bahia, Brazil. Apart from studies made in Italy and Japan, Jean-Philippe Lenclos' investigations into the changing nature of architectural colour in relation to its setting have also taken him to Brazil. This illustration results from this visit and encapsulates his complete colour analysis process. Colour notes, collected samples and on-site sketches form the basis for a range of colours which are translated into charts. The two vertical bands of colour (bottom right) represent—in cool and warm ranges—the polychromy peculiar to traditional buildings and their Bahia setting. In turn, these have been translated into elevations which display proposed colours sympathetic to the area. PHOTO: JEAN-PHILIPPE LENCLOS

materials from walls, roofs, doors, shutters and so on, together with natural parasites (mosses and lichens) and rocks, earth and vegetation are methodically accumulated. Studies are also made of changing light conditions owing to diurnal and seasonal cycles. The second phase is a long and meticulous synthesis in his Paris studio. All the samples are examined and faithfully translated into painted colour samples. These are then classified and regrouped to form 'colour maps' which describe the precise colour qualities of both a region and its architecture (**3.4**).

Phase three is the presentation of an applied colour vocabulary appropriate to each region. Two colour systems are evolved: a primary system offers a range of colours which harmonize into a given area and are intended for large architectural surfaces. A second, extended system, based on a wider selection of natural sources, including flora, is intended for use on secondary elements such as door and window frames. Lenclos' initial analysis led to the manufacture of a series of exterior paint ranges developed in order to compensate for the erosion of the traditional colours of France caused by the invasion of synthetic and alien construction materials. Lenclos' apparent success with this analytical colour approach has also led to several experiments being undertaken by him outside his native France. These have mainly concentrated on selected areas in Japan, Italy and Brazil (**3.5**).

In complete contrast to his process of integration, Lenclos has also devised colour programmes for industrial sites and apartment buildings located in nondescript settings. These have turned silos, cranes, storage tanks, warehouses and large industrial plants into colourful 'sculptures' (**3.6**). His prescriptions for the schools in Créteil and Cergy-Pontoise new towns have

3.6 Acièrie Solmer Steel plant, Fos-sur-mer. Lenclos believes that industrial forms are a natural subject for a positive chromatic statement, for industrial zones often occupy vast areas of space situated away from the context of traditional buildings. Lenclos' work with the Urbame design group on this steel plant is an example of a recent trend amongst French colourists.
PHOTO: JEAN-PHILIPPE LENCLOS

3.7 Ecole Les Maradas, Cergy-Pontoise. Lenclos felt that this school building merited a sculptural extension via colour. In conjunction with its architect, Jean-Pierre Georges Pencreac'h, the pupils and the teachers, he embarked on the idea of creating a giant spectral toy—of which this is the blue-green section. PHOTO: J. DIRAND

converted harsh concrete buildings into a brightly painted architecture for children (**3.7**). It is through the potential of colour that Lenclos aims to help us come to terms with our modern environment. Already his analysis and application methods—the latter discussed in Chapter 5—have been adopted enthusiastically as a design tool by design institutions in Europe and America, and, as part of their environmental activities, by the Japanese Colour Planning Centre in Tokyo (**3.8**).

Other French colourists

Until recently, however, the mainstream colourist movement has remained firmly rooted in France. Apart from Lenclos, two other notable exponents are Fabio Rieti and Bernard Lassus, who weave their polychromatic experiments into the fabric of existing buildings and into the design of new urban developments. Lassus is in charge of the Urban Design Research Centre which, under the auspices of the Thionville Housing Department, works on the upgrading of 23,000 dwellings within its jurisdiction. Lassus takes a different view from that of Lenclos. He is convinced that there should be no colour regulation. In defining his role, he describes himself as an 'architectural interpreter'—using colour not as camouflage, but as a means of celebrating

3.8 a and b Tokyu Abiko village apartments, Tokyo. In a country where land is at a premium, the main function of architectural polychromy is, according to the Japanese Colour Planning Centre, to aid 'a harmonious integration of high-rise forms in the landscape'. The researches of the Centre are entirely based on methods devised by Jean-Philippe Lenclos in France. The charts represent 'chromatic palettes' of analogous harmony assembled from studies of local terrain on the site of a new Tokyo suburb. The apartment tower uses four of these colours and is an example of one of the many ways in which these have been applied by colourist Shingo Yoshida to buildings in the area. PHOTOS: SHINGO YOSHIDA

3.9 Shemerten apartments, Mondelange, France. An approach to environmental colour representing the antithesis to that of Lenclos. Bernard Lassus, director of the French Urban Design Research Centre, states: 'Colour is not a cover-up.' Using around seventy colours for every square metre of façade, his intention at Mondelange is to 'dilute' mass. Here, he orchestrates colour by value so that, as the daytime riot of colour subsides into night, its tonal arrangement takes over. PHOTO: BERNARD LASSUS

its wealth of diversity. As if to prove the point his studio is surrounded by samples of 16,000 colours as a demonstration that the visible spectrum is his only constraint. From these he has applied extravagant schemes comprising eight hundred colours to housing façades in Marseilles, and seventy to apartment exteriors in Shemerten, Mondelange (**3.9**). Such an extreme reaction to the monotony of the urban scene has, generally, been confined to Europe. Further examples are the harlequin-coloured 'villes nouvelles' at Grenoble, Martigues, Liège, Geneva and, of course, the Paris satellites.

The French new town at Marne la Vallée has a downtown section which is gradually acquiring a blue appearance made up from a full range of colours in the region of that hue, from turquoise to violet and from light to dark—but always bluish. This is a project by Fabio Rieti whose 'new town blues' theme is social rather than aesthetic in motive. His idea is that its residents will come to identify themselves as inhabitants of 'Marne le Bleu' as, indeed, Verona and Algiers respectively are known affectionately to their citizens as the 'Red' and the 'White'. Rieti hopes that in an environment seemingly designed more with the motor car in mind than people (a crisis in many recent urban landscapes which must surely be followed by another), colour might help to improve the quality of life. By fostering some distinction, Rieti's blue is intended to act as a kind of cosmetic cohesion which might enhance a psychological relationship between environment and imagination.

Environmental colour in Britain: A. C. Hardy

Meanwhile, English new towns have also been the subject of some notable experiments. One which immediately springs to mind is Peterlee in County

Durham. Here, since 1954, Victor Pasmore, in prescribing his umbers, Indian reds and blues to the timber panelling of its housing, has been associated with the idea of collaboration between artist and urban designer. More recently there has been the carefully integrated colouring by Runcorn's Chief Architect, Roger Harrison, and the more unbridled use of primary colours in Milton Keynes. Also, there have been the gallant attempts of the Civic Trust who, through consultative co-ordination with house owners and shopkeepers, have succeeded in bringing some sense of order to the colours of selected High Streets.

In the U.K. a further example of the systematic investigation of outside colouring is found in the work of Professor A. C. Hardy of Newcastle University, whose approach stems from principles developed by H. L. Gloag and others at the Building Research Establishment, Hertfordshire.

Several years ago it became apparent to Professor Hardy that there was little information available to architects concerning the choice of colour for large-scale structures such as agricultural buildings, factories and bridges, etc. situated in countryside settings. As it was not possible, for practical reasons, to physically reduce their scale, it appeared that the only action possible was a reduction of their visual impact by means of appropriate surface colouring.

As visual perception studies indicated that this was a 'target-background' problem, i.e. the degree of visual interaction between 'object' and 'field' caused by varying relationships in the colours of man-made forms and the natural colours of their setting, Hardy began by analysing the visual components comprising the 'background'. The colour of vegetation, surface geology and the area of soil visible due to agricultural activity were studied under various daylight conditions and at different seasons. Unlike Lenclos' French 'regional palettes', this pilot study soon discovered that, apart from coastal and moorland areas, it was virtually impossible—due to the variety of building materials—to divide the British countryside into zones of buildings of similar colour.

This phase of Hardy's survey was recorded by Munsell Notation with reference to the Munsell Atlas—a precision system of notation first published in 1915 that enables most colours to be defined. Munsell organized colour systematically in terms of 'hue', 'value' and 'chroma' (i.e. hue, lightness and saturation respectively). Within the Atlas, *hue* defines the redness, blueness or greenness of a colour sample; *value* defines the lightness or darkness of a colour; *chroma* is the amount of colour in a hue, e.g. variations in red from the brightest to the palest pink. Each colour quality, or dimension, is subdivided by Munsell into a scaled series of decimal increments which—given numerical annotation—allow a colour sample to be specified precisely.

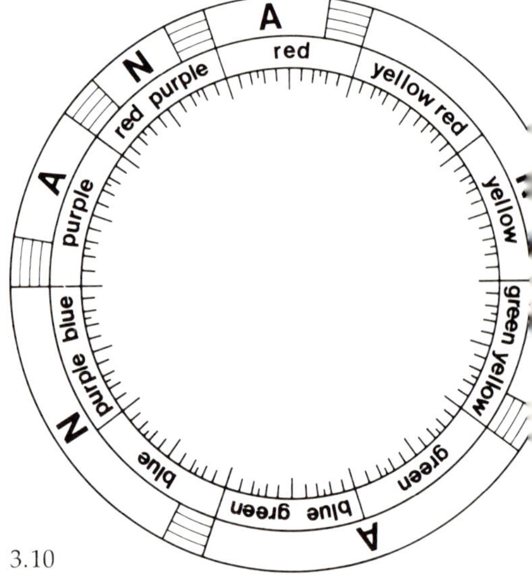

3.10

3.11

3.10 Munsell hue circle. The outer circle indicates the broad divisions of hues into categories of 'natural' and 'artificial'. Apart from some ambiguities in the Purple and Red-Purple zone, Hardy's findings were that natural ground surface colours are concentrated in the Red to Red-Yellow zone, and sky and water hues in the Blue-Green to Purple-Blue zone. The small zone of natural colour centred around the Red-Purple hue is due to heather and certain weeds which produce large areas of this hue—even when viewed at considerable distance. The surprising result is that Munsell Green does not occur naturally and therefore to colour buildings green in the landscape will not usually relate the form to its background, especially if it is of high chromatic strength.
COURTESY: A. C. HARDY

3.11 Colour contrast in the countryside. Professor A. C. Hardy believes that it is not always true that development will be detrimental to the countryside. Here he shows how a carefully coloured tower silo and farm building can be introduced into an otherwise monotonous or undeveloped landscape so that its contrast will add a centre of interest.
COURTESY: A. C. HARDY

Containing 1,500 annotated colour samples, the Munsell Atlas remains the most important colour measuring instrument in the manufacture of paints and in colour research. It is described in more detail in Chapter 5.

As Professor Hardy's study focused upon large buildings, it was restricted to the colour appearance of the countryside as seen from a distant viewpoint in which the individual hues of foliage and flowers merge into an overall impression. Initial factors investigated were the range of Munsell variables (hue, value and chroma) to be found in the natural scene, and an attempt to pinpoint 'natural' and 'artificial' hues on the Munsell hue circle (**3.10**). Brightness values were found to lie in general between value 4 and value 8 (about 12 per cent and 56 per cent reflectance respectively) on the Munsell scale of ten steps, from black at value 0 to white at value 10. Readings of Munsell chroma, or saturation, were found to be less significant than those of value because of the diminishing effect of distance. Chroma could be prominent on occasions, as with fields of mustard in full flower, but such prominence was short-lived.

The second stage in Hardy's project was the consideration of colours used for new buildings in relation to the landscape—a phase representing the shift from a study of 'background' to a study of 'target'. Hardy had noted earlier that, even when constructed from the same material such as baked earth, traditional roofs appeared darker than walls. This occurs even though pitched roofs collect more direct sunlight, and is an almost universal effect caused by macro-texture, i.e. the effect on surface colour of shadows projected from roofing elements. To this factor Hardy adds the effects of scale, shape and proportion, and their architectural subdivision by patterns of joints and connections between building materials, as having a major influence on colour decisions. These are especially important when visual 'attachment', i.e. closer degrees of visual connection between object and setting, is the prime concern of the designer.

Visual 'attachment' is not always easy because, by contrast with the colours of natural vegetation, the matt texture and horizontal textural 'grain' of a rural building tradition using stone, brick and timber, modern materials present smooth, often glossy shapes which are plain-coloured surfaces of vertical proportion. Also, experiments show that value is the most important colour decision. This is because an underlying principle of human eyesight in the handling of colour for visual 'attachment' (or its opposite) is that its attention is drawn instinctively to the brightest and most contrasting features of a scene. Both such features depend on the lightness values of the colours being used.

To achieve visual 'attachment' in terms of colour alone all three colour variables must be considered, and a comparison made with those of the background. With regard to hue, similarity with those of the background would seem an obvious choice. However, as all three colour variables in the background will vary constantly in reaction to daylight and seasonal characteristics, it is not possible to achieve a high level of visual 'attachment'—but only to minimize or maximize the impact of the buildings or other structures. When the former is desirable, it may be possible to manipulate other visual cues such as a use of matt rather than glossy surfaces or, when design features offer the opportunity, the breakdown of larger surfaces using different colours.

While rural buildings will usually be perceived against the earth and vegetation of a landscape, this is not always the case. Vertical forms are often seen in the middle-distance against the changing colour and brightness of the sky, or possibly against the sea. This presents a difficult situation for, if a building is related to the landscape, it will provide a high contrast when seen against the sky, and vice versa. In this situation, providing the building is acceptable in geometric form and its siting is compatible with other centres of attention, it may be thought wise to colour it so that it becomes a visual feature (**3.11**). The use of hues which contrast with those of both landscape

3.12 a and b Weathershield town and country colours. A selection of soil samples collected from various regions in the United Kingdom. They illustrate part of the first stage in the development of an exterior paint palette by Imperial Chemical Industries, Ltd. This kind of geographical study is a new departure in the paint industry as it is the antithesis of the creation of colour ranges that attempt to set or follow fashion. It is also linked closely with the current mood among designers who wish to integrate their architecture with the colour of its environment. Devised by Jack Widgery (Colour Consultant to I.C.I. Paints Division) and his team, the range of twenty-four colours aims to avoid colour anarchy in both town and country, enabling buildings to be colour schemed to retain and complement the character of surroundings. COURTESY: IMPERIAL CHEMICAL INDUSTRIES, LTD.

and sky appears to be most suitable and, to avoid either ambiguity or excessive contrast with the sky, high rather than low lightness values should be used. Where a vertical building creates its own visual interest, this may be enhanced by increasing the value difference between the highlight and shadow areas. Hardy concludes that, in general, black or darker colours of very low Munsell value should be avoided as they may appear as 'visual holes' in the landscape. Likewise, white should also be used with caution as this may stand out incongruously in sensitive environments.

The development of environmental paint ranges

Another British study, this time conducted by a team under the direction of Jack Widgery, Colour Consultant to I.C.I. (Imperial Chemical Industries, Ltd.) Paints Division, used as its starting point the recurrent colours of vegetation and building materials found across Britain. Integral features of local landscapes (soils, bricks, tiles, rock, sand, clay, wood, slate and thatch) were systematically studied and carefully categorized. Basic colour properties were then analysed and, much along the lines of Jean-Philippe Lenclos' French study, taken as reference points for the development of a range of external masonry paints containing twenty-four colours. This range also contains a wide colour contrast essential to the planning of successful and integrated colour combinations in both town and countryside (**3.12**).

Environmental colour in Latin America: Carlos Cruz-Diez

The opposite of seeking palettes in harmony with natural and traditional colours, as in some of the European examples quoted, is the injection of hues drawn from a cool and calculating science-inspired art form into the naturally softer palettes of South America. This is being done by Carlos Cruz-Diez, who is unique among environmental colourists. He has emerged from the world of Op Art—a form of art which exploits certain characteristics of visual perception. Much of his research has attempted to isolate the colour experience from other phenomena—extending, as well as questioning, the teachings of Joseph Albers (which were concerned with chromatic interaction within a single plane) in the multidimensions of space.

Interest in the observer–stimulus relationship, and the basic principles of colour vision have led this Venezuelan artist to embark on a variety of environmental projects in Caracas, his native city. These comprise distinctive patterns in stripes of vibrant colours deployed on many city surfaces, from pedestrian 'zebra' crossings, entire street floorscapes, buildings, buses, to a mile-long wall of colour applied to the pilings supporting a motorway which follows the bank of the River Guaire (**3.13**). By applying a geometrical pattern of strongly contrasting colours, on the lines of those used in Op Art

but to a much larger scale, he creates an impression that rapidly alters with distance as the colours merge and interact. For example, to view at close hand the vertical stripes of yellow, blue, black and white on the giant cylinders of the silos at Guaire is to experience their 'local' colours. However, from a distance their interaction induces an optical metamorphosis of their mass, which is perceived as having an ephemeral pinkish hue (**3.14**). Similarly, the intersecting blue, white and black on projects for the Simón Bolívar International Airport and railway terminal at Encanto visually warp their respective pentagonal and cylindrical forms. As the spectator moves away, they cause the experience of an ephemeral yellow—a colour not present in the original design.

In serving to demonstrate effects of colour in action, Cruz-Diez's projects centre on the two forms of visual modification inherent in the process of colour perception: first, the changing appearance of colours with change in

3.13 Wall of additive colour, Carlos Cruz-Diez. Projects such as this mark the decline of the gallery art object in favour of an environmental version which brings art into public view. In this instance, Cruz-Diez was attracted to the pilotis which support a freeway in Caracas, Venezuela. This is because they replicate on an urban scale the slatted studio constructions used as supports for his optical experiments. Apart from the stripe configuration which causes ambiguity between form and colour, movement to the left or right presents different proportions of its colours to the eye. This induced animation of the colour experience is central to the work of the Op artists. COURTESY: CARLOS CRUZ-DIEZ

3.14 a and b Silos at Guaire, Caracas, Carlos Cruz-Diez. The left-hand plate illustrates the 'local' colours used by Cruz-Diez in this project, i.e. the actual colours of paints applied to the silos. By comparing them with their impression from afar, we experience a transformation due to the additive mixing process which takes place in the eye and brain and which is caused by an interaction of blue and yellow plus black and white. The result is a pinkish-brown—a colour not present in the stimulus. COURTESY: CARLOS CRUZ-DIEZ

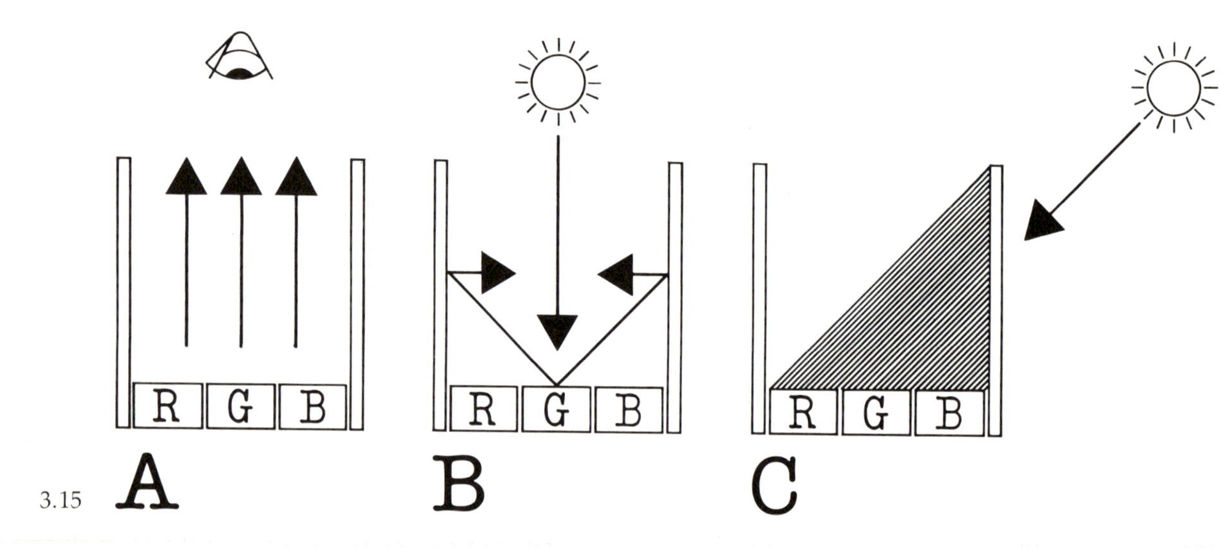

3.15

3.15 Optical colour-mixing. A diagrammatic explanation based on the experiments of Carlos Cruz-Diez. (a) *Additive colour:* the infusion in the eye of a multitude of 'isolated' hues that, in merging on the retina, optically fuse to create a new colour—each retinal mix being different when the same stimulus is viewed from different spatial points; (b) *reflective colour:* a modification of the colour of light waves which, after bouncing from one coloured surface, rebound to another, differently coloured surface to be modified and, again—if a third coloured surface is introduced—remodified, before their chromatic energy reaches the eye; (c) *subtractive colour:* the radiation into space of coloured light passing through transparent planes of colour such as stained glass. COURTESY: CARLOS CRUZ-DIEZ

3.16 Speke Hall, Liverpool. The black and white half-timbering of Tudor buildings cannot, in the strict sense of the word, be described as 'colour'. In its original state, however, Speke Hall might have been more colourfully painted than we imagine. COURTESY: THE NATIONAL TRUST

the intensity and angles of illumination (natural or artificial), coupled with change in angle and distance of viewing; second, changes due to purely optical effects in the perceptions of certain kinds of colour patterns which the artist exploits (**3.15**).

By applying his screens of colour on to different urban surfaces, Cruz-Diez engages the spectator in renewable colour experiences brought about by physical behaviour, chance movement, decisions and successive perceptions. However, the idea of extreme contrast on buildings is not new. Although its geometry is not the kind on which Op Art effects depend, the black and white half-timbering of Tudor façades is now thought likely to have been infilled with a red or yellow ochre (**3.16**). This form of high contrast was much loved and imitated by the Victorians who, in following nautical traditions of their day, first introduced their black and white appearance. This stemmed from a protective application of pitch to the timbers of Tudor buildings in coastal areas such as Avonmouth and Merseyside. The style thus developed became the prototype for a later, much maligned Tudor revival which, in the early part of this century, was to sweep over the speculative 'semi-d's' of a spreading suburbia.

Environmental colour in the United States: Foster Meagher

The effect of a naval tradition on the colours of coastal architecture can also be found in San Francisco. During the Second World War a surplus of drab grey used on wartime vessels in the Bay was liberally applied to the city's Victorian timber houses in order to camouflage their fancy fretwork and to dampen their once impressive hues. For those with short memories, this pervading battleship blue-grey is still sentimentally associated with their ornate woodwork. However, more knowledgeable owners have been moved to restore their homes to a degree which exceeds even their former glory. This colour revolution followed in the wake of sixties' 'flower power' when the spectral daubings of its rainbow children on the façades of Haight-Ashbury—adopted suburb of hippies—triggered some local designers to offer their services (**3.17**). They became colourists—consultants to those who wished to re-express the intricate beauty of their homes through a multicoloured cosmetic.

The subsequent facelift to San Francisco's architectural heritage was begun by such design groups as 'Blissful Painting', 'Flying Colours' and, a forerunner in the field, 'Colour Control'. The latter is a team headed by Foster Meagher, who describes himself first as artist, second as designer and third as colour consultant. He claims that nothing in his colour prescriptions is left to chance: consideration is given to a building's history, location and setting, the amount of sunlight it receives, its exposure to weather and the impact his

908

colours will have on the street after redecoration. In other words, Meagher suggests that his studies of a building's exterior are of the same depth that an interior designer would give to an interior space. Often, if a building façade is dull, void of architectural embellishment or character, he will continue the design assignment in paint—continuing where the architect left off. In effect, Meagher claims that, if a building due for redecoration is properly studied, even nondescript architecture can be made to appear attractive. The operation he proposes 'amounts to nothing more than opening the correct tin of paint and applying its contents to the appropriate part of the building' (**3.18**).

Within a city in which it is not unusual to find up to eighty different colours on a single façade, Meagher adopts an approach which demands that his colours perform architecturally. He considers five colour functions when prescribing schemes for façades. First, a background 'body' colour—usually of high lightness value—which occupies flat wall surfaces. Second, a colour he describes as 'architectural', i.e. one of high chroma which will delineate any visible working parts such as plinths, corbels, columns, etc. Third, individual or pairs of target colours—usually strong hues—used to pick out door panels, linear framing, mouldings, etc. Fourth, a dark colour of low value, employed when necessary as a 'shadow' to help large, unattractive areas recede. Finally, a fifth colour is also held in reserve; a colour high in lightness value used, when required, to project any additional architectural finery of note (**3.19**).

Meagher has observed that on completion of his commissioned projects neighbours and residents in other parts of the street turn to a redecoration of their own houses. Also, he shares the claim made by many European and American colourists and muralists—that a recharged environmental colour attracts tourists rather than graffitists. For example, sales of picture postcards depicting San Francisco's 'painted ladies' vie with those of the Golden Gate, Alcatraz and cable cars; also, Steiner—a complete collection of vibrant Victoriana—has become one of the most photographed streets in the United States. Meanwhile, the colour revolution on the West Coast has swept southwards to join in the fun of the Los Angeles vernacular revival, and to bring a sense of gaiety to a combination of indigenous Spanish Mission colours and a polychromatic adventure into Post-Modernism.

Much of the energy of the fast-growing colourist movement is directed against the indiscriminate coloration of architecture and the discordant and conflicting colours of throwaway commercialism. The message is simple: that true architectonic art should be a fusion of form and colour. Also, as colour is a basic element necessary to our existence, it should have a coordinated role both in existing environments and in the creation of new

3.17 (preceding page) 'Hippie House', San Francisco. This house, situated in the Haight-Ashbury district of San Francisco, stands as a monument to the psychedelic colour mood of the late sixties. It was decorated by its 'hippie' inhabitants who, using artists' brushes, applied every colour of paint they could lay their hands on. In fact, eighty different colours make up the scheme; the result became a prototype for the revival of more sophisticated multi-colours which swept the area in the seventies. PHOTO: © BY MORLEY BAER FROM *Painted Ladies*

3.18 (preceding page) Victorian cottage, San Francisco. After making several pastel sketches of her home, the owner decided that she 'might as well go all out' and have her favourite colour, purple, as part of its redecoration. Foster Meagher—head of Colour Control—did the rest, adding two reds, a dark brown and white to complete the scheme. PHOTO: © BY MORLEY BAER FROM *Painted Ladies*

environments. Certainly, in questions of environmental colour, professionals must be consulted if we are to develop visual environments which, in an increasingly urban world, enhance the quality of life. Therefore, if we accept the act of the designer in employing colour to achieve certain effects, can we not accept attempts to preserve an existing palette or, at least, encourage the colour of a new town to remain consistent with that of its setting?

3.19 House on Fulton Street, San Francisco. Built in 1875, this superb Victorian villa once housed the Imperial Russian Consulate. Foster Meagher has applied a simple but extremely effective harmony to recapture for its new owners something of its colourful past. PHOTO: © BY MORLEY BAER FROM *Painted Ladies*

4 ARCHITECTS AND COLOUR

Not only have colourists turned to the external environment but architects, too, have begun to free themselves from the design of buildings as a colourless science. Invading the greyness of post-war architecture, dominated with shuttered and prefabricated concrete, an increasing use of factory- and self-coloured building materials paved the way for more individual expression. Colours for service systems became transferred to a new role, that of identifying major structural elements. This coincided with the high-tech dismembering of form—spawning structures whose hitherto private parts are exposed. In some cases, these are show-cased behind external glazing; in others they have simply disgorged their multicoloured entrails into the street. Industrialized forms have imploded, their walls sucked in behind exposed space frames which, in requiring protection, become prime targets for colour. Meanwhile, other designers experiment with the brilliance of vitreous enamel and the subtlety of tinted glass. Other materials such as colour-mixed brickwork, plasticized stucco, anodized and plasti-coated metals, stains and colouring agents for concrete have also been exploited together with, of course, paint. There has also been the adventure into new forms made possible by G.R.P. (glass reinforced plastic) and G.R.C. (glass reinforced concrete) which, for their formulation, require a colour decision from the user.

Much of this colour display has emerged over the last two decades; its extremes performed acts of aggression, blasts of colour against lingering post-war austerity. A peacock architecture suddenly burst on the European scene. In West Berlin, for instance, the blue and pink fantasy of Ludwig Leo's University Hydrology and Engineering Building seems to intensify the drabness of its setting. Also in Berlin, the searing reds and red-blues of the colour-washed Märkisches Viertel showpiece appear to announce the coming of the colour revolution to the naked concrete of the eastern sector. French architects, quick to seize upon the successes of the environmental artists, introduced strong colour into Paris and its satellite new towns. Experiments were also happening in other parts of the globe. In Thailand, Finland and Russia (the latter not without its own rich tradition of colourful buildings) architects with one eye on the European explosion were beginning to use bolder colour on façades and to advertise the fact in their professional journals.

In England, the more gradual swing in the colour pendulum can be retraced to the transformation of paint ranges in the late fifties by H. L. Gloag and D. Medd. They were responsible for a new balanced range of forty-eight colours, published in 1953, for application to school buildings, extending from greys to strong reds, blues, yellows and greens. Against the backlog of manufacturers' ranges heavily loaded with institutional creams, greens and browns, the new range made an immediate impact on architects who adopted it for other types of building also. After this pioneer colour range came another, the first British Standard colour range designed specifically for buildings—B.S. 2660 (1957). This had 101 colours and like its predecessor was structured by means of the Munsell System.

The popularity green has had for external application is not surprising. After all, being the widespread selection of nature, it has passed the greatest outdoor 'weathering test' of all time! In the fifties and sixties an olive green thrived as a kind of army surplus khaki. By the seventies there was a fashion for a tart green and while James Stirling experimented with its combination with lilac, Norman Foster and Richard Rogers were both prescribing it for interior and exterior finishes. Ralph Erskine, on the other hand, favoured a seaweed green stain for the woodwork and his Byker backyards and Milton Keynes clapboard. In the eighties an intense viridian—used in large areas and as backdrop for rich reds and blues—has become widely associated with industrial envelopes such as those by Nicholas Grimshaw & Partners (**4.1**).

A decision to use primary colours, but this time on the exterior of a city building, was taken by Dutch architect Aldo van Eyck. In this instance, colour was used on mullions in order to arrest the diffusion of the mainly glass-faceted façade of his 'Mothers' House'—a home for unmarried mothers inserted into a nineteenth-century street in the centre of Amsterdam. Here, on a small scale, is an application of colour recalling that of Owen Jones for the Crystal Palace, i.e. to index the linearity of a tracery structure. Van Eyck's application of this colour system acts to reinforce a spatial progression from old to new and from street to building via a transitional, scooped-out entrance area which sucks public space into a semi-private zone. Here, colour plays an active role in sequencing a passage along the

4.1 (preceding page) Factory, Castle Park, Nottingham, Nicholas Grimshaw & Partners. Red and green are used here to break up the great silver slabs and make the inhuman vastness of industrial building humanly acceptable and comfortingly jolly. PHOTO: JO REID AND JOHN PECK

4.2 Mothers' House, Amsterdam, Aldo van Eyck. Enlisting spectral hues to frame his glass structure, Aldo van Eyck explains that 'although the walls are very transparent, what *is* left of the material has to be made articulate. Therefore the reds, greens and blues came in, one after another . . .'. This home for unmarried mothers is the antithesis of all that is institutional. PHOTO: PATRICE GOULET

colourful canyon; three blues articulate the street elevation and move inwards via two greens to a yellow before ascending into orange, orange-red and vermilion, crimson and black—redefining the hollowed space—through violet to the blue of the street (**4.2**). Inside, the progression continues as a means of differentiating the succession of spaces throughout the building; blues and greens become orange before a confrontation with a mixture of natural materials. Finally, a roof garden for the children: a rain-

bow of natural colours from which its young inhabitants can pick flowers and disperse their colours throughout the building. Van Eyck has described his design of this building as an architectural 'bouquet of flowers' displayed amid the dirty creams and browns of the city. Indeed, his 'floral' tribute to Amsterdam has been cited by Herman Hertzberger as one of the most important buildings of the decade.

However, van Eyck's rainbow colours were not installed without some raised eyebrows from passers-by. When the blues were first applied, consternation approached outrage as more and more hues were added. Later, as the totality of the rainbow became apparent, the architect noticed that dismay had quickly weathered into acceptance. Although van Eyck's colours were selected to comprise the clear, simple hues which children easily recognize, he explains that it was only when its 'scientific reality', i.e. its obvious reference to the spectrum, was completely apparent that it elicited general approval.

In order to further animate his building, van Eyck inserted tiny reflective strips of mirror and coloured ceramics into its support elements, such as the columns and plinth. This type of architectural jewellery can also be found in and on many buildings—with obvious roots in the jackdaw-like assembly of glittering fragments in the art of mosaic. More modern examples include the cobs of a turquoise-tinted synthetic glass dotted about the external stonework of Bruce Goff's Bavanger House in Oklahoma, Frank Lloyd Wright's architectural signature of a single square of vermilion glaze, and Debenham House in London—an Edwardian shrine to ceramic tiles designed by Halsey Ricardo.

The desire to make impressions in wet concrete is, however, epitomized in the outdoor public seating at Grant's Tomb in New York. This represents the love of a multicoloured surface encrustation and was applied by a local community art workshop. Another striking example is that monument to the non-designer which stands in a nondescript sector of Los Angeles. It was built single-handed over a period of thirty years by the Italian immigrant Simon Rodia as a tribute to his adopted country. The towers at Watts have signified many things for many people but, above all, they represent a do-it-yourself synthesis between the Renaissance-formed categories of painting (colour), sculpture (surface and form) and architecture (human space) in a single environmental statement (**4.3**). The quality of its surface immediately reminds one of the delights of Antoni Gaudi's scintillating potsherd mosaics which sheath the Art Nouveau towers of his Sagrada Familia cathedral in Barcelona. Also, between 1900 and 1914, and with the aid of nearby residents, Gaudi employed exactly the same decorative encrustations on serpentine seating. This was as part of his design for Guell

4.3 Towers at Watts, Los Angeles. Watts Towers were built by Italian immigrant Simon Rodia as a monument to his newfound homeland. PHOTO: MIKE JENCKS

Park which, as in Watts and New York, uses coloured fragments of glass, porcelain and china in a fabulous mosaic.

Also now in Barcelona is the multidisciplinary design team known collectively as the Taller de Arquitectura. At the head of this group, comprised of mathematicians, musicians and poets, is architect Ricardo Bofill—heir apparent to the organic fantasies of Gaudi and the Moorish delights of Alhambra. As part of their design philosophy, the Taller uses brilliantly coloured pigments and materials to decorate the exteriors of their many projects. The five inner courtyards of Walden Seven, for example, are dressed in glazed skins of orange and blue tiles which make a spectacular contrast with the earthy pigmentation of its outer shell (**4.4**). Another is an apartment building

4.4 Walden Seven, Barcelona, Spain, Taller de Arquitectura. Ricardo Bofill here revives Moorish traditions in the patterns of azure blue tiles which clad and 'cool' each of the cathedral-like spaces.
PHOTO: SERENA VERGANO

4.5

called Xanadu—an architectural echo of the shape of a nearby rocky outcrop standing in the Bay of Calpe, with its green exterior further increasing the similarity between apartment building and rock.

Close to Xanadu is yet another apartment complex which is probably the most dynamically coloured in Europe. As its name implies, La Muralla Roja is painted in a blood red on the outside, with colour progressions through to its central blue courtyard; attendant courts are pink (**4.5**). Elements such as staircases, bridges, retaining walls, etc., which fall outside the system, are coloured purple and blue (**4.6**). As a further refinement of this system, the reds, blues and purples are each used in four different tonal values, from dark to light. Recesses into the main wall surface are painted darkest of all; the surface itself is one step lighter and the balconies, which project farthest, are painted the lightest of all.

In this particular version of the Taller's colour approach one is reminded of the system of emphasis used by the ancient Greeks for underlining visually the faceted planes of triglyphs on temple friezes. However, the influences on the Taller's work also resemble those which exert such a profound effect on the work of Mexican architect Luis Barragán. His extraordinary articulation of form and space by colour has been described as being inspired by a mixture of his visit to Alhambra and his love of Moroccan architecture combined with the Mexican tradition.

4.6

4.5 La Muralla Roja and Xanadu, Spain. Two buildings which represent extremes in colour function. On the one hand, La Muralla Roja uses sharp, contrasting colours and form to detach itself from its setting; on the other, the Gaudi-esque curves and earthy green of Xanadu correspond with the local landscape and its colour in the heat of the summer. PHOTO: SERENA VERGANO

4.6 La Muralla Roja (*detail*). As a further refinement to the progression of parent colours, Bofill's reds, blues and purples are each used in four different tonal values, stepping from dark to light. These are applied wherever projections or penetrations occur in the main plane such as in window frames, balconies and some staircases. PHOTO: SERENA VERGANO

Almost all of Barragán's buildings are small houses, apartments and, especially, ranches which are confined to his native country. His breathtaking sense of colour is, not unnaturally, deeply founded on a feeling for the sensual palettes associated with a traditional South American culture. His masterly handling of pinks, purples, ochres and red oxides on walls surrounding patios and courtyards creates colourful outdoor rooms (**4.7**). As at Alhambra, a sensation intrinsic in Barragán's spaces is that added dimension provided by the presence of water. Apart from watering livestock, his pools, fountains and channels mirror and refract haunting pigments which are carefully deployed to define one plane as it overlaps another. Under the brilliance of Mexican sunlight the colours annually succumb to the ravages of ultra-violet light. However, in a culture where a springtime redecoration is a celebratory ritual rather than a chore, this is not viewed as a problem; rather a cyclical recharging of a life-giving property.

Both Barragán and Bofill have discussed their love of paint in terms of a necessary 'skin' which, when applied, allows forms to 'breathe', thereby bringing their architecture to life. To the purist designer such a philosophy smacks of too much cosmetic; indeed, it is nicknamed by critics as '2mm architecture'. However, the fact that a layer of applied paint can bring so much spatial animation and so much visual delight to the experience of

4.7 San Cristobal Riding Academy, Mexico, Luis Barragán. A dreamlike stage-set in which the horse is actor. Horses enter and leave the training enclosure through openings cut into the long pink wall, while riders and grooms make their appearance quietly from behind the double layers of the purple wall. Barragán's colour celebrates intense sunlight. Earth pigments are applied in the knowledge that they will be consumed by the sun and in the acceptance that, like a ritual, they must be periodically repainted. PHOTO: ARMANDO SALAS PORTUGAL, COURTESY RUDER & FINN, INC.

4.7

buildings otherwise cold and undistinguished is answer enough (**4.8**).

Barragán's and Bofill's colour schemes are both devised under the same sparkling sunlight which illuminates the palettes of towns and villages in South America and Spain (**4.9**). In these drier latitudes colours can benefit from a lighter ground surface which increases the amount of reflected light. The combined effect of both direct and indirect sunlight intensifies architectural colour—a condition experienced in more northerly climates when the perception of colour is enhanced by a ground-cover of snow. The changing effects of a colour response to a particular quality of light can be found in the more obvious differences in colours used by artists when paintings produced in different climatic regions are exhibited together. Architecturally speaking, a similar transplantation of colour began in the fifties when migrating families of East and West Indians began to settle in the industrial centres of the U.K. They brought with them their love of bright

4.8

4.8 House of Luis Barragán, Mexico. It is interesting to note that Barragán's feeling for colour is rarely evident on the drawing board. It is confined exclusively to his imagination, and only realized on the ultimate architectural form as here in a colourful 'outdoor room' in his own house in Mexico City. PHOTO: ARMANDO SALAS PORTUGAL, COURTESY RUDER & FINN, INC.

4.9 House in La Esmeralda, Cumana, Venezuela. This basic yellow and blue scheme is typical of the striking combinations used traditionally on houses in Venezuela and throughout Latin America. In brilliant sunlight a high contrast between colours is employed as a means of pattern-making while exploiting architectural elements. PHOTO: GRAZIANO GASPARINI

4.9

4.10 House in Rochdale, Lancashire. By comparison with the intensifying effect on colour of the sparkling light in the southern hemisphere, the clouded skies of the north—plus a darker groundcover—tend to dull the chroma (chromatic strength) of colours outside. In this example, newly arrived Pakistani immigrants have redecorated the outside of their home without taking this effect into account. In a greyer climate, successful colour combinations have to rely even more on a well-handled contrast between the lightness and darkness of colours.
PHOTO: DOUG SARGENT & GRAHAM COOPER

colour and transferred this as a kind of brush-applied sunshine to the façades of their newfound homes (**4.10**). This decoration at first appeared chromatically unbalanced, for in the context of cooler, cloudier environments with darker ground-cover the chroma of colour dulls.

After the initial shock wore off, however, this colour profusion influenced indigenous residents to use more brightly coloured paints for external decoration. This shift in taste coincided with that of a younger generation of British architects, already mentioned, who were experimenting with more saturated colours on the insides and outsides of their buildings. A similar shift of emphasis toward higher levels of colour saturation in external decoration also occurred in America. The leading American colour consultant, Faber Birren, attributes this to the gradual erosion of a prejudice which equated strong colour—considered to be emotionally rather than intellectually judged—with a distraction from form. He suggests that this may be irritating to some designers, i.e. that the effect of a coat of paint may be more compelling than the edifice it covers. Generally, apart from homes, much of exterior American architecture has been off-white, grey-brown and bronze-brown for, before the arrival of Pop Art, colour had not been a central design issue. There were, of course, exceptions, such as Frank Furness' painted cast-iron, and in the imported Mediterranean colour-splashes of José Luis Sert.

The seventies witnessed an emergent group of architects, among them the Post-Modernists, who began re-experimenting with colour by engaging it as an important facet of their design. This initially occurred on the West Coast where Joseph Esherick used strong colours to introduce a territorial legibility to the façades of low-income housing projects and, in a design for a private house, Charles Moore used seventeen shades of earth colour on its stuccoed forms (**4.11**). Meanwhile, in a more northerly light which demands a well-handled colour contrast, Chicago architect Stanley Tigerman paints his curvilinear forms in sharply defined primary hues. His Illinois Regional Library

4.11 Burns House, California, Charles Moore. Set in Santa Monica, near Los Angeles, the Burns House illustrates Charles Moore's love of combinations of ochres, oranges, reds and mauves; a colour scheme he later used to effect on the Piazza d'Italy in New Orleans. However, the Burns House is notable because of the extent of the range used, for there are about twenty different colour variants of the parent range applied to its exterior walls. PHOTO: OLIVER BOISSIERE

4.12 Regional Library for the Blind and Physically Handicapped, Illinois, Stanley Tigerman. Departing from the dignified austerity usually associated with the public library image, Stanley Tigerman borrows the hues of a machine aesthetic. Apart from visually detaching his architecture from that of its setting, his colours enlist high contrast between their values in order to provide a structural 'diagram' for its users, i.e. orientation cues for the partially sighted. Tigerman's colours also herald the colours of the library interior where the salmon pink, deep blue and bright yellow act as guiding elements throughout circulation routes. PHOTO: HOWARD N. KAPLAN © HNK ARCHITECTURAL PHOTOGRAPHY

for the Blind and Physically Handicapped uses colours motivated by a deeper concern than the mere indexing of major architectural components. His concept of creating a brilliantly coloured external and internal system for a library for the blind is not as incongruous as it at first appears. Indeed, Tigerman offers a rational explanation for his choice: first, that the legal definition of blindness does not necessarily imply total loss of vision—a partially sighted person can often, through a haze, perceive contrasts among colours; second, that his saturated colours function as a challenge to that facile sentimentality with which the disabled are often regarded. Tigerman's colours certainly break with the dignified austerity usually associated with institutions and public libraries (**4.12**). A closer look, however, explains the code for the whole building: a red for exterior walls, bright yellow for the structural system, blue for ducting. The wall which forms the hypotenuse of the triangular plan is left in exposed concrete with openings and doors picked out in a contrasting black (**4.13**).

To all intents and purposes this is a harmless coding system, a machine

4.13 Regional Library for the Blind and Physically Handicapped, Illinois. As a foil to Stanley Tigerman's finely tuned 'industrial' colours, the side wall of his library is left in raw concrete and pierced with an undulating window. Vivid colour is restricted to the entrance area and car park elevation. PHOTO: HOWARD N. KAPLAN © HNK ARCHITECTURAL PHOTOGRAPHY

aesthetic to which others such as Piano & Rogers and Hardy, Holzmann, Pfeiffer have subscribed with provocative and well-published results. However, here, as in the work of Aldo van Eyck, is something more than just a use of aggressive industrial colour. Reds tend toward pink, yellow to orange, and blue to purple. It is these subtle discrepancies which give away something in the work of both Tigerman and van Eyck—a sensitive 'tuning' of hues almost hidden beneath the obvious connotations of a colour-coded system. These colours, in fact, assert what Tigerman and, indeed, van Eyck would not—that they simply exist for pleasure!

Apart from his architectural practice in New Jersey, Michael Graves is also a prolific and accomplished artist, whose painting stimulates his work in environmental polychromy. In his projects it is intimately bound up with his philosophy of form, in that both make symbolic references to other themes. For instance, Graves states that the classical origins of form have thematically derived from two things: nature and man. The floor is ground, ceiling sky, columns trees. At the same time, the orders are derived from the partitions, symmetry and geometry of the human body. The classical language of colour, on the other hand, is derived only from nature and nature's materials, not from man; for example, the green 'meadows' painted on the floors of Egyptian temples, and the blue 'heavens' applied to medieval vaulting. Graves explains that, although colour is two-dimensional, our understanding of it is in terms of the three-dimensional. He suggests that: 'No matter how one might know colour to be an application to a surface, we see colour first as representational. To some degree, therefore, it possesses the quality of an object, an artifact.' It is this aspect which fascinates him, and in his work it becomes an extra ingredient that makes reference to other periods, materials and ephemera.

It is in this sense that Graves' thesis subscribes in part to that of Faber Birren for, by assigning symbolic meanings to his architectural palette, he uses their potential to full effect (**4.14**). This 'language' of colour can be found in his remodelling of the Schulman House which, if subjected to a cursory glance, merely registers as a wall painting extending the limitations of a physical architecture (**4.15**). A second, more searching look, however, reveals a veritable catalogue of colour references which echo elements that lie within, on and beyond its envelope, while others recall historically what might have been.

The paint on the gable of the existing house makes direct reference to an architectural genealogy: the white echoes the stone surface of its neo-classical roots; the yellow symbolizes the colour of stonework which might have existed to define entrance and chimney. It is this particular function which reminds one of Italian *trompe l'oeil* façade decoration, where paint was

4.14 Addition to Benacerraf House, New Jersey, Michael Graves. This extremely well-balanced colour composition, using a strategic panel of red as the centre of attention with space-frame delineations of blue, green and yellow against a background of white, has a distinct fine art genealogy. COURTESY: MICHAEL GRAVES

4.15 Schulman House addition, street façade, Michael Graves. Michael Graves uses paint to extend the modelling of his extension to an existing clapboard house. Here, 'wallpainting' becomes architecture, with a layer of paint being substituted for changes in materials and form. PHOTO: © EZRA STOLLER ESTO PHOTOGRAPHICS INC.

4.16 Schulman House addition, garden façade. Michael Graves' use of green on the garden elevation simply explains that this side of the house acts as an extension of the garden and vice-versa. PHOTO: PETER AARON ESTO PHOTOGRAPHICS INC.

applied as a cheap substitute for expensive building materials and exterior ornamentation. However, the functions introduced to Graves' extension for the Schulman House exist for other reasons. Here, bands of different colours are assigned to establish a dialogue between 'inside' and 'outside'. The deep green band skirting the base is painted in order to 'plant' the building in its garden setting; the lighter façade green mirrors its relationship with the grounds—yet another green used on the garden wall is 'borrowed' from a nearby tree. Two horizontal clay-coloured stripes denote 'ground'—the two different floor levels within the building—while an elevated blue architrave denotes 'sky' (**4.16**).

4.17

4.18

4.17 Lang House, Connecticut, Robert Stern and John Hagmann. Ornament was banished in modern architecture but is revived by the Post-Modernists in a new way. On this house, white trim mouldings wander about, sometimes connecting up windows, sometimes dividing a storey in two rather than one floor from the next. Another moulding pops up over the front door, symbolizing the formal entrance. Traditional forms are also distorted; the yellow symmetrical façade is meant to recall Palladian country houses. PHOTO: ED STOECKLEIN

4.18 Casa Papanice, Rome, Paolo Portoghesi and Vittorio Gigliotti. Its architects explain that their colours on the Casa Papanice carry on a 'dialectic with nature'. Over a mostly white façade, glass mosaic stripes of green 'emerge' from the undergrowth and, together with an earth brown, travel skyward. These alternate with blue stripes which 'descend' from the heavens. All are mixed with ribbons of gold which bring 'light' to a colour modulation set amidst the monotonous panorama of modern Rome. PHOTO: OSCAR SAVIO

4.19 Elementary school, Asti, Paolo Portoghesi and Vittorio Gigliotti. In comparison with the vertical lines of the Casa Papanice, the horizontal colour bands of this school brace the white, prefabricated form with green (grass) at the base, gold (light) at its middle, and blue (sky) under the eaves. Bound up in the symbolism of Portoghesi and Gigliotti, and also in that of Graves and Stern, is a movement towards 'natural' colour. COURTESY: PAOLO PORTOGHESI

Colour conversations between a building and its history are also an aspect of the work of the New York architect Robert Stern. In his design process colour plays a similar Post-Modernist role in contriving adjustments in scale and chasing decorative elaboration. His bicoloured scheme for the house in Connecticut—Lang House, designed in conjunction with John Hagmann—uses contrast in value to separate trim from façade. It also plays a historical game by nudging the memory into recalling a mixture of past architectural images (**4.17**).

In the course of history, colour has been used instinctively to alter the appearance of size, shape and form. During the Renaissance it was not uncommon to use horizontal lines of red, orange and deep yellow to give the illusion of added width to buildings. The use of stripes is also thematic in the design work of architect Paolo Portoghesi, who, like Graves and Stern, handles colour to make obvious and sometimes overt references to nature and the past. A dialectic with nature is found in Rome on the tesselated curvilinear shell of the Casa Papanice, co-designed with Vittorio Gigliotti (**4.18**). Here, lines of colour denoting sky, grass, earth and sunlight are woven into a vertical rhythm. This theme is continued, this time horizontally, on the prefabricated elementary school in Asti. In conjunction with mouldings, vari-coloured bands brace the mainly white elevation. The cerulean of the upper strata attempts to pull the colour of the sky on to the building, while the lower sequence draws its pigmentation from the earth; the central viridian, as in the Schulman House, reflects the colour of evergreen foliage (**4.19**).

From such examples we realize that a concept of exterior colour has, among many leading architects, become re-established as an important aspect of their architecture. Only now does colour as a design tool seem free from the restriction of nineteenth-century dogma and the guarded restraint of the early twentieth century. In making good its escape, environmental colour is no longer subject to those stringent rules which had tended to inhibit its widespread use.

4.19

5 MAKING COLOUR DECISIONS

5.1 THE PERCEPTION OF COLOUR

In practice we work with colours and materials that reflect wavelengths, but the colours we see do not exist on the surface for they are manufactured in the mind's eye. Our experience of colour is a subjective sensation conveyed through the medium of these wavelengths, i.e. energy in the form of light radiations within the visible spectrum. Without an observer, light rays do not, in themselves, constitute colour. As Sir Isaac Newton was careful to point out in his *Opticks*, '. . . the rays to speak properly are not coloured. In them there is nothing else than a certain power and disposition to stir up a sensation of this or that colour'. The eye and brain of the observer interpret the meaning of these sensory messages. The resulting experience depends upon three important factors: the lighting conditions under which colour is viewed, the spectral characteristics of the object in view and our perception of colour.

The lighting conditions

Despite *visual adaptation* (the automatic adjustment of the eyes to prevailing levels and colour of illumination) artificial light sources may sometimes cause perceptible alterations of object colours as compared with their appearance in natural daylight. This occurs when adaptation cannot fully compensate for the differences in the spectral energy distributions of the two light sources. It is this initial factor that presents a golden rule when making colour decisions, viz: colour selections should always be made or tested under light sources similar to those specified for the final scheme. Too often an architect will specify under fluorescent lamp illumination the colours of paints and other building materials destined to be seen in the strong light and shade of natural daylight. Variation in illumination accounts for the sometimes astonishing distortion of coloured artwork produced under tungsten light when viewed in daylight. Each colour perception responds to the two different spectral energy distributions in each light source, indicating the need for the designer, if not working exclusively in daylight, to fit colour-matching lamps in his studio. Also, when more than one lighting condition will be encountered, as in combinations of artificial and natural light, it is important to consider the effect of both sources in advance.

The effect of latitude on the changing effect of light explains the marked difference in colour applications between designers in the northern and southern hemispheres (discussed in Chapter 4). It also accounts for artists' stereotyped preference for studios lit by the more even colour-rendering properties of northern light, and for the regional emphasis placed by designers such as Jean-Phillippe Lenclos and A. C. Hardy on a copious study of the ultimate settings for their colour prescriptions. For example, Lenclos insists that the designer should be aware that environmental colour is a dynamic element, subject to a constantly changing perception. He states: 'Although a building may reflect the same range of colour as its mineral environment, its colour is not static. It evolves, shifts and changes seasonally as a result of changes in light, air, humidity, rain and drought.'

A further consideration concerns the day–night cycle and the threshold of illumination below which colour cannot be seen. This can be demonstrated if we imagine the impression of a red sign painted on a white building viewed in moonlight. As night turns to day we would be able still to read the sign's letters in very low levels of illumination, but the daylight has to increase quite considerably before the sign is perceived as red. This is embodied in Bernard Lassus' coloration of the panels of the Shemerten Apartments at Mondelange on which the tonal value of his 800 colours was designed to continue entertaining the eye as an organized achromatic pattern when daylight (and therefore the colours of the façade) had subsided.

The spectral properties of the object

The second factor of colour vision depends on the spectral characteristics of the object—the ability of its substance to absorb, reflect or transmit light. Red paint, for instance, generally appears red because it has the property of absorbing from the incident light less in the red than in other parts of the spectrum. In working with a gamut of materials, the architect controls space using surfaces and finishes with varying abilities to absorb, reflect and transmit light. This brings us to another golden rule when prescribing environmental colours: self-coloured materials such as exposed concrete, brick and wood, etc. should not be looked upon as neutral backgrounds to colour schemes, as each of these materials reflects colour! For example, the

5.1 (preceding page) Identity harmony in action. The choice of a colour scheme based on a single hue is, of course, the safest route to providing architectural colour harmony. Such schemes involve the exclusive exploitation of chroma and value to induce colour change. The Taller de Arquitectura's La Muralla Roja in Spain contains a sequence of mini-essays in the use of identity harmony. This staircase, for example, is composed of different value versions of the same blue. They are used to define horizontal from vertical and, therefore, intensify form. Behind it, tones of light and mid-blue are used more traditionally to separate frame from wall plane. PHOTO: SERENA VERGANO

colours of all non-luminous materials are perceived by the colour of the light they reflect. Matt surfaces and matt paints reflect diffusely, scattering light waves in all directions, regardless of the direction from which they came. Polished surfaces and gloss paints, on the other hand, reflect specularly: each reflected light wave making the same angle with the surface as the incident light wave (in other words, it reflects straight back to the observer). Colours, therefore, will look darker and more saturated when reflected from a glossy surface than they are when reflected from a matt surface. Also, a colour on a heavily textured surface such as shuttered concrete will appear darker than the same colour on a smooth surface.

A further aspect of our normal everyday experience of colour, however, is that, when associated with objects, it retains its identity under a wide range of lighting conditions. This phenomenon, called 'colour constancy', results from our past association of colour with different objects; an orange, for example, will be accepted as 'orange-coloured' even when its colour impression is modified by differing light sources.

The sensation of colour

The third factor in our perception of colour is the chromatic sensitivity of our personal technicolor processing laboratory—the eye and brain. In reaching the eyes, spectral energy stimulates light-sensitive nerve cells in the retina known as rods and cones, the messages from which are conveyed to the brain via the optic nerve. The rods are sensitive to light and not to colour, giving only perception of white, grey and black. They are sensitive to very low levels of light and virtually go out of action at high levels of illumination. The cones are the colour receptors; they operate at higher levels of illumination and are responsible for our ability to distinguish chromatic colours.

The idea that colour is seen in the brain is verified by experience of colour with our eyes shut, as in dreams. The existence of our personal colour processing laboratory is further exemplified by the incidence of *anomalous colour vision,* popularly misnamed 'colour-blindness'—the most common anomaly causing confusion of reds and greens.

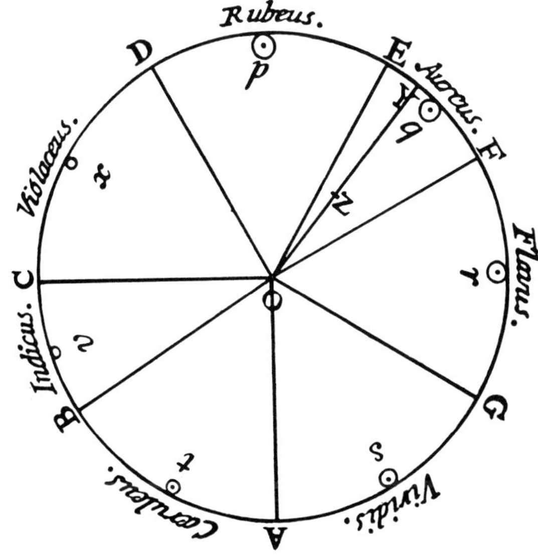

5.2 Sir Isaac Newton's colour circle. The first colour circle, invented by Sir Isaac Newton around 1660, resulting from his experimental work with light and colour.

The development of colour theory

The search for a theory to account for colour occupied the Greek philosophers as early as the fourth century B.C. Aristotle, for example, observed all colours as a darkening influence on light—a theory which fits Isaac Newton's theory of white light radiating all the spectrum, and all colours, whether of lights or objects, radiating parts of the spectrum only. The year 1660 saw a breakthrough when Newton produced the first colour circle by simply joining the two ends of the visible spectrum (**5.2**). Attempts to systematically organize surface colour dimensions gained impetus in the nineteenth century with Goethe and Chevreul, and in the early twentieth century with Ostwald and Munsell—outstanding among theorists who sought to classify the gamut of surface colours. Before discussing the geometry of colour dimensions, however, two processes of colour mixing should be examined. This returns us to the two external components of the colour vision operation: the properties of light and of surface, or object.

Additive and subtractive colour mixture

The process of mixing patches of coloured light is sometimes called *additive colour mixture*—a process first brought to light by Newton's celebrated experiment using a prism to split a beam of sunlight into the visible spectrum, and another to recombine the colours into white light. In the second stage, Newton found he could also obtain white from mixing only red, green and blue, a discovery which was later enlarged by the work of Thomas Young (1801) and others, and expanded in 1867 by Herman von Helmholtz and others into the Young-Helmholtz Theory. This proposes that the colour receptors in the eye respond to red, green and blue wavelengths of light, a theory widely accepted by physicists and adopted almost universally by scientists for their measurements of colour. The three primary colours used for colour photography and colour television also stem from this theory. A rival theory by Ewald Hering (1874) proposes three pairs of colour receptors (red-green, blue-yellow, black-white). This theory has many supporters in Europe and in the U.S.A. and has been the basis of certain German and Swedish atlases, beginning with Ostwald's.

As distinct from mixing light to achieve colours, *subtractive colour mixtures* occur when pigments, dyes, colour filters and, indeed, paint for the coloration of buildings, are mixed. For example, when two paint colours are admixed, the resulting colour experience is created by energy wavelengths common to both. It is called subtractive because, when mixed, the spectral energy of one pigment will usually neutralize parts of the spectral energy of another. If yellow, blue and red, the subtractive primaries, are mixed they neutralize each other to produce grey.

The Munsell system of colour notation

From among those who have attempted to chart the world of subtractive colour, Albert H. Munsell's system of colour notation is the most useful to designers. His method of notation arranges the three attributes of colour into calibrated scales of equal visual steps. These scales are used as dimensions or parameters for the accurate analysis or description of a colour under standard viewing conditions.

5.3 Related hue symbols arranged on the Munsell 100 hue circuit. As part of his colour system, Albert H. Munsell devised his hue circle in 1915. Any one of several symbols may be used for the notation of hue. The initials for the ten major hue families (shown in the inner circle) may be used alone for the approximate identification of hue. Numerals from 1 to 100 (shown in the outer circle) may be used alone for the cataloguing of colours. The combination of numerals with the hue initials (shown between the inner and outer circles) is considered to be the most accurate form of hue notation.

5.4 a and b Munsell colour space and colour solid. The Munsell scales of hue, value and chroma can be visualized in terms of a colour space or a colour solid. In the colour space (left), the neutral value scale, graded in equal steps from black to white, forms the central, vertical axis. The hue scale is positioned in equal visual steps around the neutral axis. Chroma scales radiate in equal visual steps from the neutral axis outward to the periphery of the colour space. The Munsell colour solid (right) is shown with one quarter removed in order to show the plane of constant hue 5Y. Its irregular shape accounts for the extended chroma scales along those hue planes with increased saturation such as red and yellow-red, etc. The value scale, on the other hand, is limited by its poles of perfect black and perfect white (both not achievable in material form). As with the hue circle, however, chroma and value scales may be subdivided by the use of decimals into increments as small as required for more accurate colour notation.

The colour dimension of *hue* is the attribute of colour discernible by its redness, blueness, greenness, etc. In the Munsell system 100 hues are arranged in spectral sequence around the perimeter of its colour circle (**5.3**). This number results from a decimal subdivision of its ten (five principal and five intermediate) hues: *Red*, Yellow-Red, *Yellow*, Green-Yellow, *Green*, Blue-Green, *Blue*, Purple-Blue, *Purple* and Red-Purple. For the general identification of a hue the use of its initials is adequate notation; for a more critical specification, numerals from 1 to 100 can be used either with or without hue initials.

Munsell's colour circle occupies the middle of his three-dimensional model of the world of colour, the ten hues representing its equator. Its central, vertical axis represents the second colour attribute—*value* (or lightness). This occurs as an achromatic scale which descends in ten equal steps from absolute black (value 0/) at its base to absolute white (value 10/) at the top (**5.4a**). The centre of this scale—located at the core of the colour solid—is occupied by a mid-grey with a notation of 5/.

Chroma (or saturation) refers to the intensity of a colour, i.e. the amount of colour in a hue. Chroma scales radiate in equal decimal steps from the neutral axis outward to the periphery of the colour model. Increasing steps of chroma are indicated in Munsell notation by degree of departure from the neutral grey of the same value (**5.4a** and **b**). Chroma scales extend from /0, for

5.3

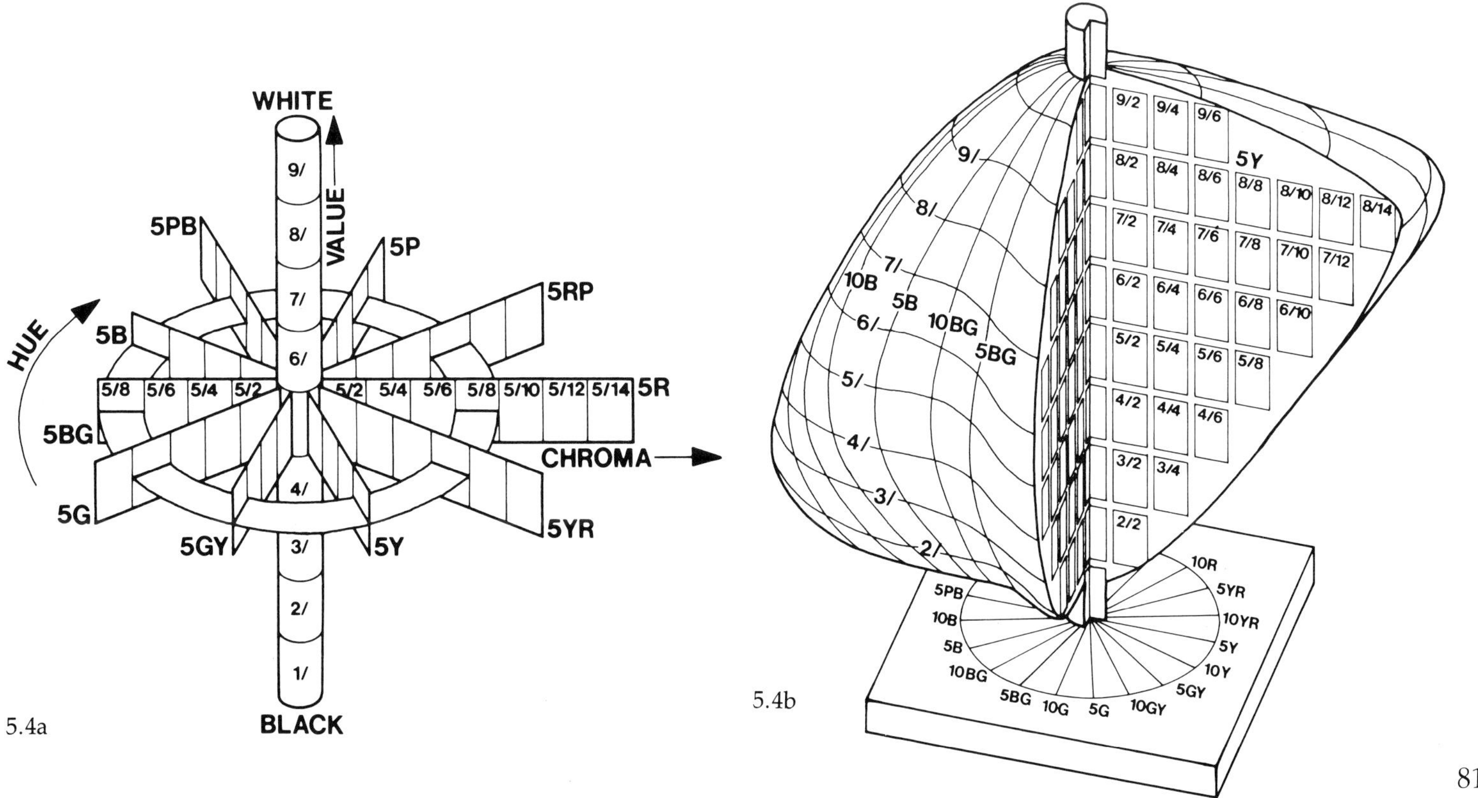

5.4a

5.4b

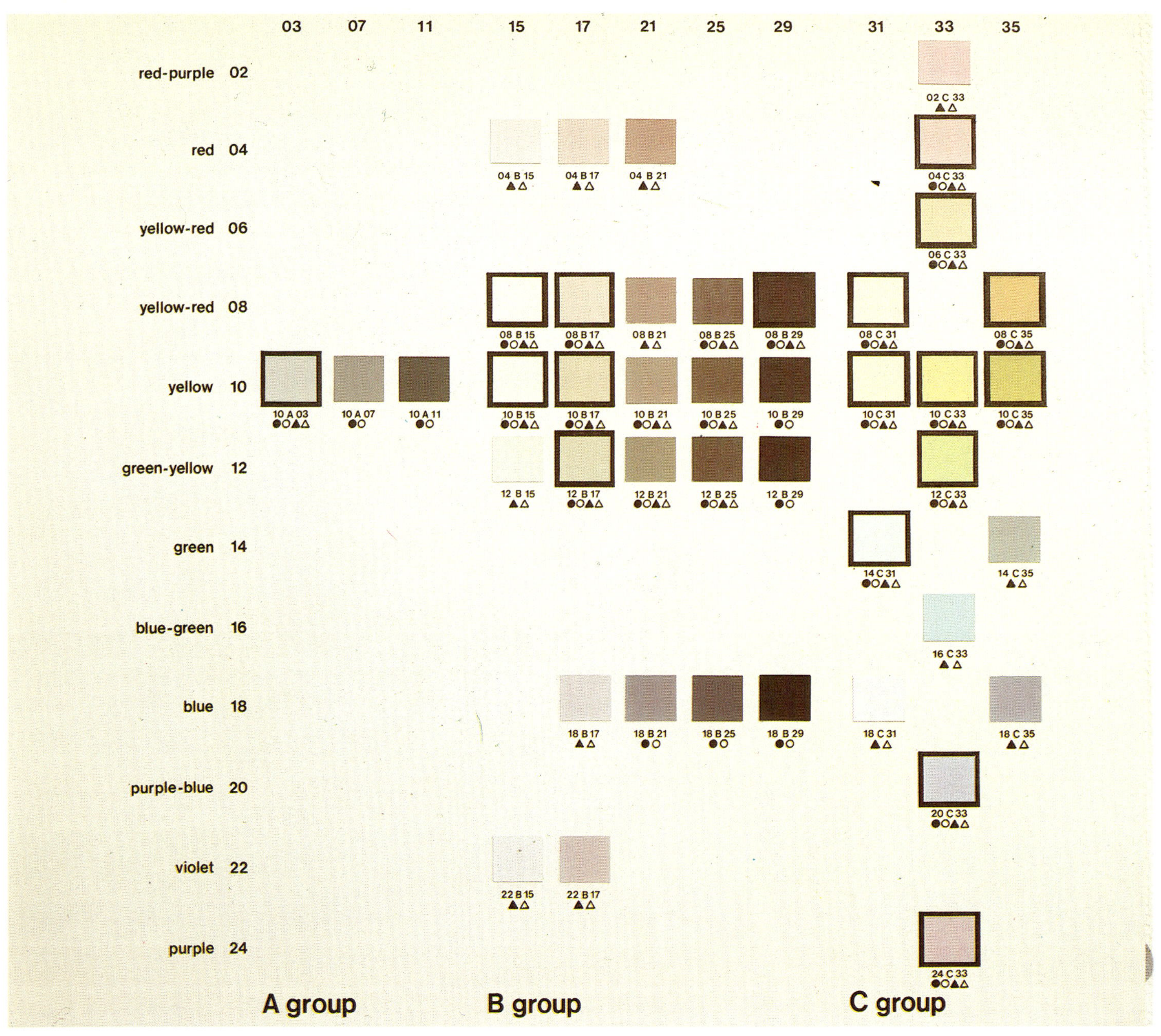

5.5 B.S. 4800:1981 Paints colours for building purposes. This chart represents in modified form the 1981 revised version of B.S. 4800 which is a specification for paint colours and their finishes. Like its predecessor, B.S. 4800:1976, it is derived by the British Standards Institution from their existing framework of 237 colours contained in B.S. 5252—a parent framework for colour co-ordination for building purposes from which other standards, such as those for external cladding, plastics and vitreous enamel, etc., have also been drawn. The colours are arranged within this framework along scales of hue, greyness and weight: greyness denoting the grey content of a colour, i.e. its saturation level, weight being used as a subjective term for lightness. For example, this framework includes twelve horizontal rows of hues plus another (not shown) for neutral colours. These are divided into five vertical groups

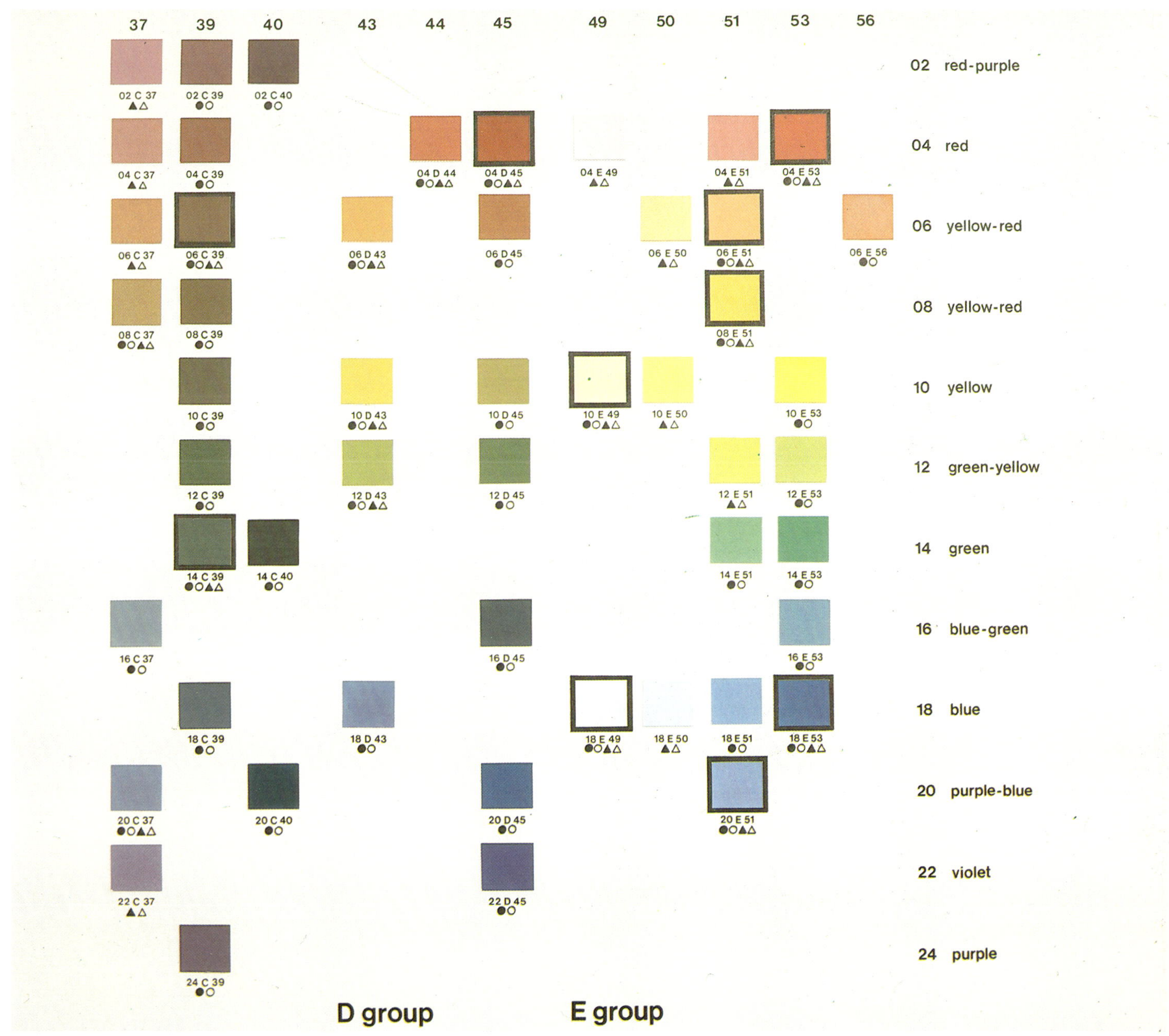

lettered A to E—each representing steps of diminishing greyness. Within each group there are up to eight vertical columns of equal weight, ranging from lightest on the left to darkest, or heaviest, on the right. Specification of these scales is reflected in the three-part coding for each colour; the first two numerals identify its hue, the middle letter signifies its greyness, and the second pair of numerals identify its weight.

This adapted version of the B.S. 4800:1981 framework was prepared with the help and kind permission of the British Standards Institution. It does not include all of its 100 constituent colours, and no claim is made for an accurate representation of the colours shown.

a neutral grey, out to /10, /12, /14 or farther, depending upon the saturation strength of a colour sample. For example, a bright red might be rated as /12 but a more vivid version can be designated at /16.

The complete Munsell notation for a chromatic colour is written symbolically: Hue Value/Chroma. The complete notation for a vermilion, for instance, might be 5R 5/14. However, when a finer division is required, decimals are introduced, for example: 2.8R 4.5/12.4.

Applications of the Munsell system

A knowledge of colour space and its notation is of considerable importance to the designer, for the creation of environmental colour schemes relies upon the selective control of the hue, value and chroma; contrast among them acting as the key to their success or failure. The ability of the Munsell system to describe colours accurately along measured progressions, therefore, makes it an invaluable design tool. In presenting over 1,500 detachable samples of colour in matt and gloss finishes, the Munsell Atlas allows quick comparison among varying degrees of colour relationship. This also accounts for its widespread use internationally by designers, colourists and researchers such as Jean-Philippe Lenclos and A. C. Hardy, for identifying or selecting colours according to qualities of appearance both in the field and in the studio. It also accounts for its use in colour specification such as in the Turin restoration programme headed by Giovanni Brino. The Munsell Atlas is further adopted as a colour measuring instrument by bodies such as the U.S.A. Bureau of Standards, the Japanese Industrial Standard for Colour and the British Standards Institution. Under the chairmanship of H. L. Gloag of the Building Research Establishment, a committee has developed the British Standard framework for colour co-ordination (B.S. 5252) which is wide enough in scope to act as the source of colours for a series of derived standard ranges, such as that for paints (B.S. 4800) and other coloured building materials. The research behind this framework led to the introduction of 'hue', 'greyness' and 'weight' which are modifications of the Munsell dimensions with clear advantage for design purposes (**5.5**).

Colour harmony and disharmony

As part of an ability to communicate and use colour effectively, the designer should be able to distinguish between harmony and disharmony on a reliable basis. To take account of colour harmony in the structuring of the framework for co-ordinating the colours of building materials later embodied in B.S. 5252, the Building Research Establishment reviewed the literature on colour harmony including propositions by M. Chevreul (1879), W. von Bezold (1876), A. H. Munsell (1905), W. Ostwald (1931), P. Moon and D. E. Spencer

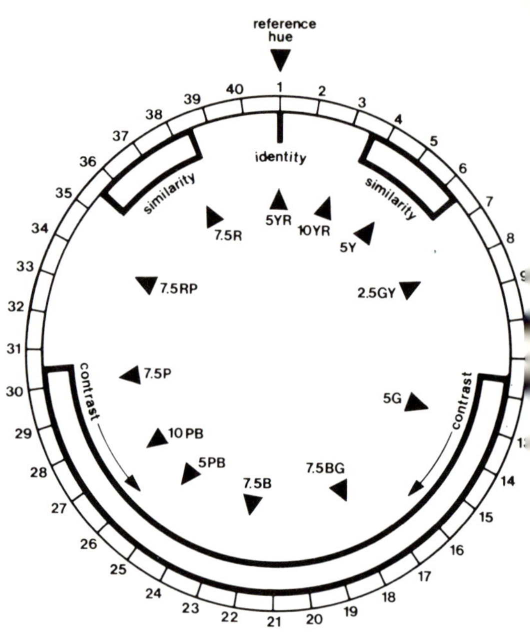

5.6 Identity, similarity and contrast harmony. Moon and Spencer's three categories of harmony separated by the zones of ambiguity on a 40 step Munsell hue scale. This diagram was devised by the Building Research Establishment after an exhaustive review of literature dealing with colour harmony. It shows the relationship between one of the main hues (5YR) adopted for the colour co-ordination framework in B.S. 5252 and the other eleven. If each of the twelve hues is taken in turn as the reference hue, each will be in similarity or contrast harmony with at least seven others. The B.R.E. stress two general points: that experience in using the Moon and Spencer sectors suggests that the transition from one sector to the next is gradual rather than abrupt; and that the sectors represent only a broad classification of hue relationships and to this extent have positive practical value. This figure is based on data published in P. Moon and D. E. Spencer's 'Geometric Formulation of Classical Colour Harmony', *Journal of the Optical Society of America*, 1944, and represented by and reproduced from Figure 11 in the B.R.E. *Colour Coordination Handbook*, 1978 (Crown copyright) BY PERMISSION OF THE CONTROLLER, HMSO

(1944) and Rudolf Arnheim (1954). No single set of rules for harmony emerged but the work of Moon and Spencer seemed the most penetrating and helpful. Using Munsell notation, Moon and Spencer proposed three sorts of unambiguous colour harmony: 'identity', 'similarity' and 'contrast' (**5.6**).

'Identity' refers to colours of the same, or nearly the same hue—as with a monochromatic harmony. In this type of colour combination a series of colours, all derived from one hue but with well-spaced chromas and values, are found to be harmonious when put together (**5.1**). 'Similarity' in colour harmony refers to colours linked by having a shared hue, e.g. yellow and green-yellow, or red and yellow-red. This kind of harmony has sometimes been termed 'analogous' (**5.7**). The third type, 'contrast', refers to colours of

5.7 Similarity harmony in action. This design for the concrete exterior of apartments in Klarenthal, a small town outside Wiesbaden, was devised by the German colourist Friedrich Ernst von Garnier. Garnier works almost exclusively in two and three hue-based harmonies. In this example, the tonal value of his green, green-yellow and yellow comprise a similarity harmony deployed in shapes that describe illusions of recession and projection in the façade—his attempt to 'personalize' each living unit within the mass. PHOTO: FRIEDRICH ERNST V. GARNIER

distinctly different hue, i.e. drawn from a wide segment of hues on the other side of the hue circle from the reference hue. This kind of harmony is possibly the most interesting because it can be used to enliven the effect of a group of more closely related colours (**5.8**). In between these sorts of harmony are regions of ambiguity, or 'discord', where the relationships with a given hue are indefinite and clashing.

Gloag's conclusion is that while the subject of colour harmony remains controversial, the Moon and Spencer propositions offer useful guidelines for the designer; noting that, in practice, detailed selection of colours must depend ultimately on the designer's skill and imagination. How far harmony and disharmony will work together in a scheme for colour outside is for the designer to reflect. It is tempting, but dangerous, to draw analogies between colour and music; suffice to note that in Mozart's 39th Symphony, for instance, there is striking use of disharmony to lead into and emphasize the harmony of certain themes.

Colour phenomena experiments

The findings of colour research at large (much of it conducted within the confines of the laboratory) have confirmed many of our common stereotypes. For example, we associate certain hues, such as reds, with concepts of warmth, heaviness and an advancing aggression; blues, on the other hand, appear cool, lightweight and passively recessive. Warm colours, however, via interaction with other, warmer colours can be made to appear as 'cool', and cool colours can appear 'warm' when adjacent to other, cooler colours. In similar ways, warm colours can be made to recede, and cool colours advance. The basic reason is that hue alone does not determine the spatial position of colour; contrasts of value and chromatic intensity are equally important and frequently the controlling factors. This is exemplified by the striking effect of a colour of mid-value appearing dark against a light background, yet light against a dark background. It is from such experiments that we learn that colour concepts are relative terms, and when a number of colours are involved, it is the intervals between them which determine their temperature or spatial position in relation to one another.

Studio experiments can also demonstrate colour phenomena such as 'negative after-images', e.g. the experience of a 'mirage' of bluish-green when averting the eyes after staring intently at a small patch of bright red paint. This is thought to be caused by the previous stimulation of the red-sensitive cones in the eye which, once the stimulus is removed, triggers an involuntary firing of those which respond to its complementary colour, i.e. the blue-green found opposite on the hue circle. It is this double-acting perception that forms the basis of E. Hering's 'opponent-colour theory'.

5.8 Contrast harmony in action. Contrast harmonies involve the juxtaposition of a hue, or range of hues, that occurs roughly opposite to the reference, or parent hue on the hue circle. However, it is important that the proportion of the reference hue remains predominant in such types of colour relationships. This example illustrates the effect of a contrast harmony based on two hues designed for Phase One of the Farrell/Grimshaw Partnership Advance Warehouse development on the Gillingham Industrial Park. The two hues were carefully selected by the architects and applied in a gloss paint especially colour-mixed for the project. PHOTO: JO REID AND JOHN PECK

When complementary colours such as blue and yellow are placed together, the characteristics of each hue are intensified by the presence of the other in the visual field. This modification of judgement by colours found opposite each other on the hue circle is termed 'simultaneous contrast'. There is also 'successive contrast', a phenomenon caused by the alternate perception of differing colours found opposite each other on the hue circle. In this experiment, the resulting negative after-image induced by one visually heightens the colour impression of the next.

Colour phenomena and the design process

Such colour experiments place emphasis on training the eye to see how colour behaves relatively and to demonstrate that an understanding of colour interval is very important to colour prescription; they are also designed to stretch the imagination. However, phenomena such as after-images and successive and simultaneous contrast tend only to occur significantly when viewed in extremely small patches of either isolated or juxtaposed colours. Although they have little effect in the built environment, it is important that the designer be fully aware of them because they can adversely affect judgements of both individual and groups of colours. This is because the environmental design process usually occurs at small-scale on the drawing board—the very scale at which these phenomena operate. For example, one of the basic problems of designing for the built environment at small-scale is that apparently successful and subtle schemes can be created with small swatches of colour and materials that may be ineffective when enlarged to full size. Colours might appear too strong or too weak in the space in question. Variations in the size of colours is an important design aspect for, up to a certain size, the larger the visual area of colour the more saturated it will appear. This phenomenon makes it important to prescribe schemes from colour samples large enough to offer an accurate impression of the colours they represent.

The difference between the increased saturation of a colour on the wall and a colour on a paintmaker's chart also brings us to the effect simultaneous contrast can have on decision making. This form of colour interaction points to the importance of placing colour samples side by side when comparing them, as any difference between them will tend to be exaggerated. It also shows why the colour of a background may influence judgements of the colour of a sample, such as the white card against which paintmakers' ranges are presented. The use of a lightish grey background for colour cards and the assembly of site palettes would lessen the effect. For this reason, a grey background is used in the presentation of the British Standard colour cards. But until systematic research into this colour-change–size phenomenon is initiated, many designers will continue to work from the large, borderless, 230 × 560mm colour sheets or the looseleaf wallets or detachable booklets of colour produced by several paint manufacturers for use by architects, interior designers and colour consultants. In order to further short-circuit the perceptual problem of change in colour size, many designers, having narrowed the area of selection, find it advisable to test large samples for lighting and spatial conditions. This is done by applying a sample range of colours directly onto a representative section of the façade as a preliminary check. This and other methods will be discussed in the third part of this chapter.

Meanwhile, definitions of form and space by combinations of colour depend upon a planned use of contrasting colours with particular regard to their contrasts of value (lightness). It is to a practical design application of colour based on this key dimension that we now turn.

5.2 A PRACTICAL APPROACH

Although the territories from which each kind of colour scheme are drawn are easily plotted within a colour solid, an infinite variety of chromatic expression awaits the adventurous designer. In prescribing colour for architectural space, he reorchestrates light, using the reflective properties of colours and the intervals along their dimensions to emphasize or modify impressions of form and space. On buildings, for example, colour can be used to intensify the boundaries between planes—or individual planes accentuated by having their silhouettes outlined by one colour against another at the edges. Undulating or indented planes might receive the palest of pastels to lighten their surface and reveal shadows where dark colours would tend to conceal them. On the other hand, saturated colours set against others more subdued might be deployed to show up details, adjust the visual position of a plane, combine with others to change its apparent shape, or be injected simply to bring a powerful stab of colour to a finely balanced scheme.

Central to any selection of colours in combination, however, is the need to orchestrate carefully the intervals between the saturation and lightness levels of the various colours. As part of his colour course at the Bauhaus, Johannes Itten would always set the project of asking students to place a painted sequence of ascending greys between black and white. He observed that the inclusive number of steps in this achromatic exercise averaged about seven. At the end of their course, he would also set the same project, this time finding that students' ability to define more sophisticated scales had, at least, trebled. For Itten the increasing breadth of these scales represented a development in an appreciation of value, which he saw as the key to an understanding of colour organization. For artist–teachers like Itten, together with Joseph Albers and Paul Klee, the understanding of colour interval along all three dimensions of colour and of the perceptual effects so controlled was imperative and the recognition of this relationship is embodied in the approach of many designers to environmental colouring.

The design process of Jean-Philippe Lenclos

A process of decision making in terms of colour interval is illustrated by the consultancy work of Jean-Philippe Lenclos. He approaches the act of colour selection as, initially, one of developing a tonal base-pattern that is derived directly from the fenestration of the architecture in question. Firstly, it is important to reaffirm that any experience of colour is the product of its content, i.e. we see colour in association with other colours, forms and

5.9 a and b Les Linandes Housing, Cergy Pontoise. Jean-Philippe Lenclos' decision to use an analogous colour harmony on this housing complex designed by Jean-Paul Viguier and Jean-François Jodry was based on his sympathetic response as a colourist to the sculptural quality of their architecture. In this instance, his colour prescription is purely

spatial. On one level, it attempts to intensify the position and shape of its planes and openings; on another, it brings—through increasingly deepening value—a chromatic climax to the urban gateway at its middle. PHOTOS: PATRICE GOULET AND JEAN-PHILIPPE LENCLOS

surface textures. Each material, be it brick, concrete, steel or timber, has colour, and a close scrutiny will reveal hundreds of variations in hue, saturation and lightness. When introducing different materials to the design of architectural space we invariably articulate a variety of changing colour—in this sense, our experience of colour is constantly and simultaneously modified by a supplementary experience of all the other visual elements in the field of view. In other words, colour is texture, form and space, for we perceive each of these elements as a facet of all the others. Similarly, a building—in visual terms—is never experienced in isolation; it is perceived within its wider setting. Within this broader field of vision any ultimate effect of colour is entirely subservient to its tonal pattern—a pattern regulated by degrees of contrast among each of its constituent colour values. It is recognition of this pattern that Lenclos considers fundamental to chromatic expression in architecture.

Lenclos' approach involves other key questions. How large are the relative areas that are to be coloured? How many colours are to be used in the scheme? How often are the colours in the scheme to be repeated? These initial considerations concern the proportion and scale of the built forms, i.e. the size, shape, surface quality and degree of three-dimensional modelling of those parts to be painted in relation to those parts which are not. During this studio phase, Lenclos works on scaled elevation drawings using black ink and an achromatic range of artist's paints in order to assess the pattern—or the potential pattern—of a façade. In preparing the way for later colour decisions this graphic analysis usually explores three approaches: (i) the expression of pattern inherent in the design of the building; (ii) the development of its inherent pattern through additional tonal contrast not present in the existing building; (iii) the introduction of a completely applied pattern which might alter radically the impression given by the building. This approach is illustrated by three different projects undertaken by Lenclos.

The first was worked in conjunction with architects Jean-Paul Viguier and Jean-François Jodry, who designed a linear planned housing development in Cergy-Pontoise known as Les Linandes. Lenclos' preliminary study of the layering of planes which dominated its elevation pattern was to convince him that any future colour application should reinforce this inherent 'sculptural' quality. However, apart from his plan to stress this quality, Lenclos also recognized that colour could be used to identify more clearly the configural arrangement of the 450 dwellings in the development. This arose from the fact that, situated on a hill, the length of Les Linandes could be seen in its entirety from the main approach. In this instance, Lenclos' studio investigation, using a scale of greys between black and white, produced artwork that established a strongly contrasting tonal pattern accentuating the wide variety of indented vertical and horizontal features in the façades. Darker ranges of value emphasized the central, taller sections of the elevation which, in gradually lightening steps, moved progressively outward to the left and right extremities of its descending mass.

The next stage began a process of colour selection based on the established achromatic tonal pattern. Lenclos began by collecting samples of earth from the immediate site area; also making a study of the colours of paints and materials used more widely on the buildings of the new town. The two resulting colour charts, comprising studio-painted and colour-matched samples made from the actual samples collected in both studies, were then combined into one representative of terrain and architectural colours. This became the source for the scheme to be used on Les Linandes. A predominance of a particular type of red ochre and yellow ochre indicated the basic hues of an analogous colour harmony. This was extended by reference to the colour map into a wider range of related colours. These comprised umber, sienna, orange, and paler versions of the parent hues. Next began the task of assigning colours from this range to the established tonal pattern of the elevation—each colour being modified when necessary to match its recipient area of value in the achromatic masterplan. Lenclos' early idea of steps of pale value moving inwards from each end of the elevation and gradually darkening into a central 'climax' was respected in terms of colour. Apart from responding to this primary rhythm, lighter colour values always emphasized projecting balconies against a darker background wall plane. Also, depending upon the value contrast offered by their surrounding colour, window

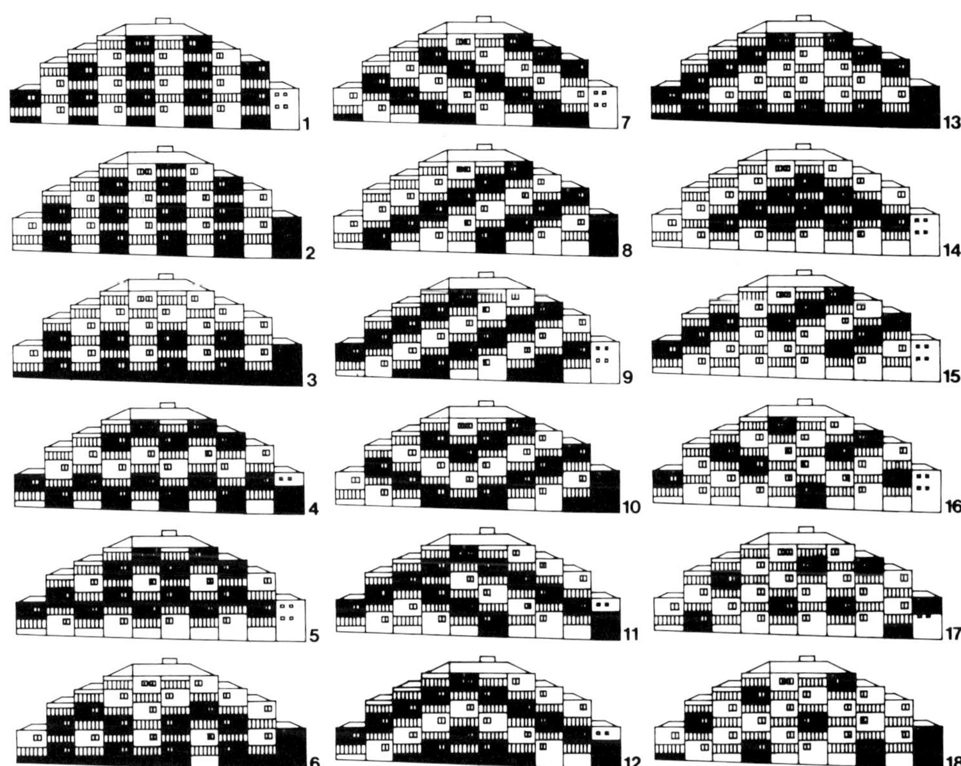

5.10 Basis for colour decisions, Chateau-Double, Aix-en-Provence. Lenclos' preparatory black and white drawings examine the potential of the underlying tonal pattern of the architecture in question. This sequence of ink drawings explores different graphic methods of disrupting the regularity of the pyramid-shaped apartments designed by Siame & Besson. After this stage, Lenclos next introduces steps of grey between the black and the white—the number of achromatic steps being directly related to the degree of contrast required in the overall scheme. Finally Lenclos begins the translation of his tonal pattern into colour.
COURTESY: JEAN-PHILIPPE LENCLOS

and door frames were picked out in either white or bright red. The colours of Les Linandes act as a splendid example of Lenclos' expertise; they are essentially uncomplicated. The progression of contrasting value steps in the colour harmony both respects the architecture and provides a continuously changing impression (**5.9**).

A second design stance is represented in Lenclos' colour prescription for eight pyramid-shaped clusters of cubic dwellings designed by architects Siame and Besson. This housing development is known as Chateau-Double and is situated in the ZAC region of Aix-en-Provence. At the outset of the project, Lenclos again quickly realized a need to undermine with colour the repetitive and aggressive geometry of their silhouettes by an emphasis on selected parts with their staggered forms. He also recognized a need to express—using a secondary system of colour—the identity of each apartment and, at the same time, make subtle connections among them. At first, Lenclos' achromatic evaluation in the studio graphically explored the idea of subdividing the clusters, using the housing units as value steps. This included the creation of bands with vertical, horizontal and diagonal emphasis, together with chevrons, chequerboard counter-changes and random alternations in tone (**5.10**). These supergraphic designs were then translated into more closely related scales of grey before transformation into scale model form. Then, the dynamic potential of each design was studied from different viewing angles simulating eye level before a final selection was made for conversion into colour and subsequent application to the eight buildings.

Before making any colour decision, Lenclos again turned to a study of the soils on and around the site area. This, and the resulting colour maps painted in the studio, suggested red ochre and yellow ochre as a starting point. However, by comparison with the ochres at Cergy-Pontoise, those at Aix-en-Provence are both richer and deeper in chroma in the red, while the hue of the yellow variety appears more green. These qualities were exploited along darkening and lightening scales of value in order to produce a scheme with enough colour 'steps' and enough value contrast to both separate the individual units visually and define the overall shapes of Lenclos' superimposed design. The later application of colours to the forms of Chateau-Double is another superb illustration of Lenclos' work. Here, more closely knit harmonies than those used at Cergy-Pontoise remedy a weakness in the physical form by disrupting its regularity and picking out each of its composite forms (**5.11**).

5.11 Chateau-Double Apartments, Aix-en-Provence. The starting-point for Jean-Philippe Lenclos' colour selection was the predominance of distinctive red and yellow ochres in the immediate site area. A value range, dictated by the tonal scale, was developed during the achromatic design stage and assessed in graphic and model form. This included closely related value steps so that a subsequent colour translation and ultimate application to the cubic units would, without losing a sense of the overall mass, visually detach one from another, following the prescribed patterns devised during the initial design stage. In placing priority on the development of a tonal base for colour prescription, Lenclos' approach is in accord with that of many colourists including Lassus and Hardy. PHOTO: JEAN-PHILIPPE LENCLOS

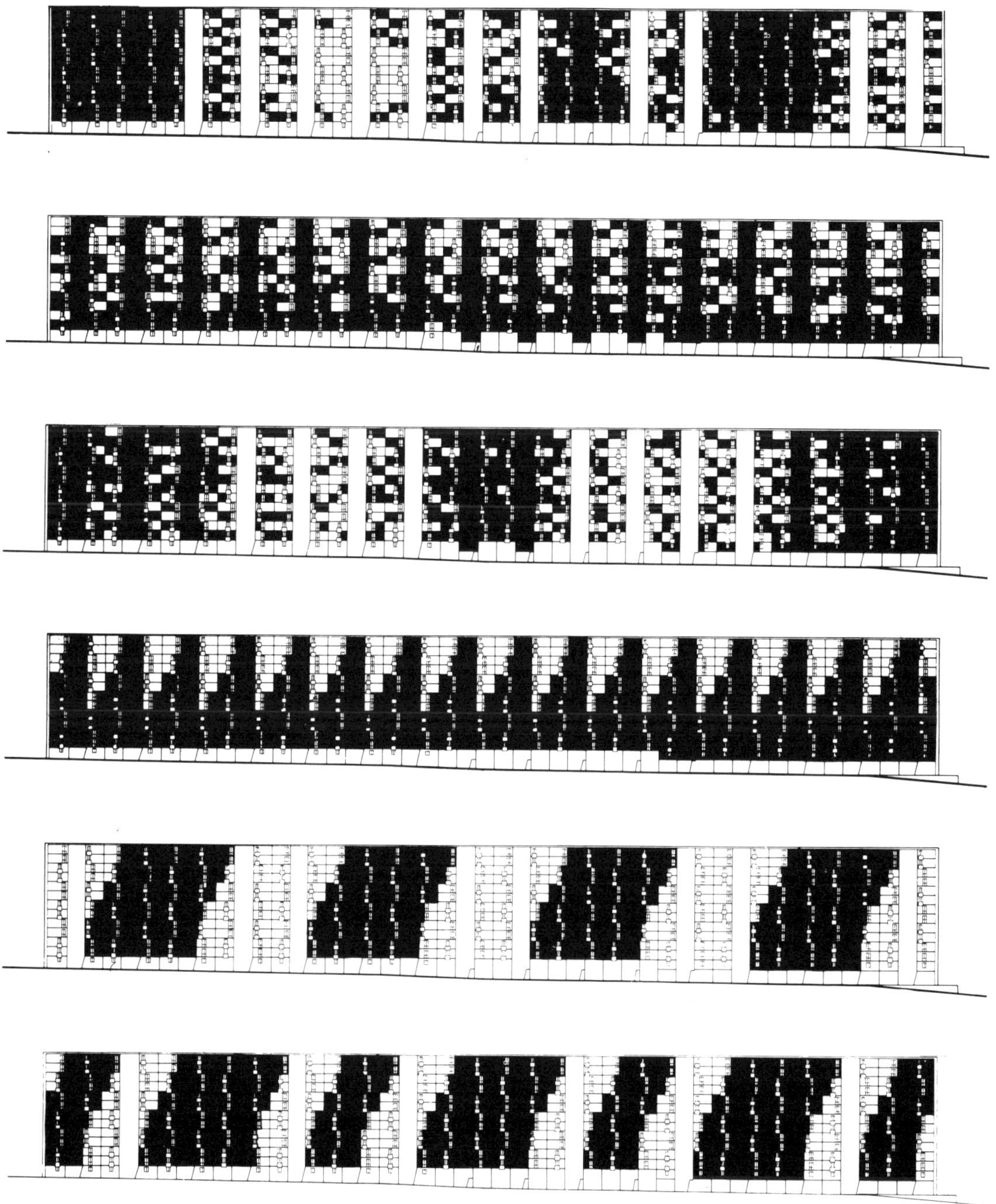

5.12 Basis for colour decisions, Campagne-Lévèque, Marseilles. This set of black and white patterns is part of a graphic sequence designed by Jean-Philippe Lenclos in collaboration with the Urbame design group. It is the basis for colour proposals for the exterior renovation of four massive housing blocks built in Marseilles during the mid-sixties. The units of proposed insulation cladding acted as the key to this approach. Its module was interpreted by Lenclos as a grid into which a whole range of figure–ground patterns exploring vertical, horizontal and diagonal rhythms could be 'woven'.
COURTESY: URBAME

Another project by Lenclos, this time worked in collaboration with the Marseilles-based design group, Urbame, shows how bland architecture on a monolithic scale can be transformed. Urbame was invited to suggest colour ranges for paint application to a proposed layer of insulation cladding—planned as part of an upgrading exercise for the existing façades of four large housing blocks built some fifteen years ago. These are at Campagne-Lévèque in Marseilles, with elevations 264 m long and 35 m high. Faced with such a daunting task, the group began by experimenting with the notion of designing large murals as a means of attacking the monotonously regular features of the housing blocks. This idea, however, was later abandoned in favour of a basic design attitude which responded exclusively to the grid caused by the joints in the proposed cladding modules. Lenclos describes this grid in terms of a mesh into which a seemingly inexhaustible series of 'tapestry' patterns could be interwoven. Using only black and white, these patterns could modify the appearance of the façades in seemingly endless variations (**5.12**).

Extreme contrast between the black and white was later reduced by artwork utilizing an undulation of value steps. Their alternate lightening and darkening progressions received a value-matched range of saturated spectral hues (**5.13**). Here strong colour was proposed as the means of distracting the eye from the predictability of elevations. Armed with such a wide variety of

5.13 Colour proposals for Campagne-Lévèque. Lenclos here introduces colour after the development of patterns in black and white. Primary and secondary hues of a high chromatic strength were utilized to attack the regularity of fenestration elements. These were either arranged in spectral sequence as shown here or, depending on the pattern used, organized into combinations using value as the motivating colour dimension. COURTESY: URBAME

pattern options, Lenclos suggests that—if the project had not been abandoned—the final integration of a colour range and its pattern could have involved the choice of residents.

Lenclos' method of starting with colour-tones seems to work well as a basis for the design of architectural colouring. His recognition of value as the key colour dimension when handling colour schemes is, despite differences in philosophy, central to the design processes of the many architects and designers discussed thus far. Once the tonal components of the pattern are decided, chromatic ranges can then be considered for integration into the system. The architecture itself, either directly or indirectly, dictates the degree of contrast between colour intervals.

5.3 METHODS AND MATERIALS

If the environmental designer is to be concerned with colour he, like the artist, should work in and therefore think in colour. Also, if the role of colour is to be a vital aid to architectural intent, then it should be considered seriously from the very outset of any urban design programme. In support, Le Corbusier made the following plea in a paper written for students entitled 'If I Had to Teach Architects'. He wrote: 'Here is a golden rule. Use coloured pencils. With colour you accentuate, you classify, you disentangle. With black you get stuck in the mud and you are lost . . . Colour will come to your rescue.' Le Corbusier's plea was made against the background of a pre-war design process that operated in, and published itself with, black and white illustrations—an achromatic means of visualization and communication which has done more to dull our image of architecture than have the elements. Furthermore, the practice still lingers, a hangover from the tradition that architecture is conceived colourlessly on the drawing board. However, an important factor that separates those architects discussed (quite apart from their striking use of colour in architecture) is their preoccupation with colour throughout the process of design. This begins with a concern for setting, necessitating an initial investigation made on and around the sites of both proposed and existing buildings.

The site survey

Whether a colour scheme is planned for a small house, a factory or an apartment complex or, indeed, a new town, and whether situated in town or countryside, it is important to visit the immediate area in order to gather information regarding its quality of colour. This is because a building or a group of buildings is never perceived in isolation but in conjunction with other man-made materials and natural forms, and observed under the prevailing conditions of light.

The basic method for colour documentation is to make a sketch plan of the site area on which the location and extent of predominant building materials and applied paintwork is recorded schematically—in other words, all colours that will have a direct bearing on subsequent decision making. Most designers, however, find that this information is better annotated on elevation drawings. These are in no way attempts at works of art. Instead, their function is either that of diagrammatic blocks of colour or outline sketches colour-rendered on-site to document a proportional representation of existing colours. One aspect of the analysis of Jean-Philippe Lenclos is worth reiteration at this point. That is the physical collection of colour samples from the site in the form of soils, fragments of building materials, flakes of paint, vegetation and any other natural or synthetic substance whose colour affects that of the site. This is done to check on the actual, or 'local' colour—an important issue because prescribed colours are usually not selected from spatially modified sources but from the precise 'local' colours of tablets arranged in a paint manufacturer's colour chart.

Some designers opt to short-circuit the site analysis by recording the area with a camera loaded with colour film. Although better than no survey at all, this method also short-circuits human vision, with the resulting danger of misinforming the eye through distortion in colour processing. Sketching is so important because it reinforces observation together with the fact that there is no truer colour-responsive instrument than the human eye.

The scale and setting of Lenclos' investigations (a preliminary to his coloration of French new town development) means that his prescribed colours can be seen from some distance. This dictates the way he documents colour: sketching from vantage points outside the site, then focusing upon selected existing buildings within the study area. By contrast, Foster Meagher focuses on individual houses in the San Francisco street context. He therefore concentrates on the recording of colours on buildings adjacent to and immediately opposite the building to be coloured. In both cases their respective analysis demands the use of mediums sensitive to the accurate colour-mixing and rendering of observed colours. When documenting on-site notes, Lenclos finds the portability and sensitivity of coloured pencils to be ideal; their interaction with the surface of drawing paper allows both subtle modulation and the rendering of flat areas of colour. Colour mixing is achieved by superimposing cross-hatched layers of different colours applied in open-mesh strokes so that the earlier strokes read through the upper layers. On the other hand, Meagher prefers to use pastels which, although less stable, have a similar rendering ability to coloured pencils but with an increased potential for sensitivity. Many architects, however, are skilled in the use of diluted watercolour and ink washes. This accounts for their preference for this medium in site surveys, and it is a medium which, using superimposed films of transparent wash, can be used to record the most delicate of perceptions.

5.14 Chromatic palette, Okinawa. As part of their survey of landscape colours on the islands of Okinawa, the Japanese Colour Planning Centre replicate the methodical analysis devised by Jean-Philippe Lenclos. Colour notes and samples collected from a proposed development area are translated into charts with reference to the Munsell Atlas. COURTESY: JAPANESE COLOUR PLANNING CENTRE

Having collected site notes, the next stage (especially if coloured elevations have not been produced) requires the compilation of gathered material into a useful form of reference. In Lenclos' case, this means the assembly of two 'chromatic palettes'—charts composed of studio-painted colour plates which faithfully reproduce the colours documented on site. One classifies the precise colours of existing buildings; the other, the natural colours found in the area. For small-scale work, however, a simple and efficient chart can be assembled quickly from colour-matched hand-painted tablets. When dry, these can be cut to shape and mounted with aerosol spray adhesive directly on to a gridded backing sheet. This might also be a chart comprising differently sized colour plates, each constituent colour responding proportionally to its area of incidence on the site. A variant on this stage is used by the Japanese Colour Planning Centre in their preparatory studies of naturally occurring colours in potential development sites in Okinawa. At the studio analysis stage, collected samples are identified by reference to the Munsell Atlas. These are then colour-matched by hand and mounted into reference charts (**5.14**).

The transfer of samples and notes into colour plates should be undertaken in daylight or a colour-balanced illumination. For this transferal, the opacity of water-based gouache (designer's colour) or tempera makes it the most suitable medium. This is because it is easy to render, its impression in artwork simulating that of external paints because it is intended to be applied to paper as an opaque skin of pigment. To achieve this opacity it should be mixed, before use, to a consistency resembling that of thin cream. As gouache tends to dry to a lighter version of its colour than when wet, it is always a good idea to check a colour-mix on a scrap of paper before any critical application. Also, the retouching of newly rendered washes should be avoided, as these can be corrected by overpainting a second wash when the first is dry.

For the beginner a basic palette of gouache would be: White, Black, Cobalt Blue, Emerald Green, Cadmium Yellow, Cadmium Red, Yellow Ochre, Raw Umber, Burnt Sienna and a Purple. 'Artist' quality pigments represent a higher quality colouring medium whilst the 'Student' quality and the Poster variant (the latter obtainable in liquid, powder or tablet form rather than in tubes) are less refined and therefore less reliable mediums.

5.15 Burano analysis, Jean-Philippe Lenclos. The range of techniques employed in Lenclos' investigations are demonstrated in this example of a project conducted in Italy. Fragments of collected materials and flakes of pigment, together with on-site sketches executed in coloured pencil, lead to the compila-

Decision-making techniques

The results of the site survey, whether in schematic plan, elevation or colour chart format, can now be used as a reference against which colour combinations for existing or future buildings can be made. During this stage it is important to visualize proposed schemes on paper first. The elevation serves as the quickest method for this purpose and should be drafted as a pencil or pen outline drawing produced to a scale large enough to accept adequately the selected medium for rendering and also to allow colour judgements of the smallest building elements to be made. One useful method when dealing with existing buildings is to trace the outlines from a photograph. If required, the tracing can be enlarged on the drawing board by either using a pantograph or by the grid enlargement method. The latter simply involves superimposing a grid over the master, then transferring the outline of the façade square by square into a larger version of the same grid on the drawing board. When dealing with proposed buildings, design or production elevations on tracing paper negatives should be dyeline printed on to the thicker print papers which accept liquid colour without wrinkling. A further consideration during the production of the elevation is the inclusion of buildings or landscape which occur to either side of the subject architecture. These are then rendered in their appropriate colours and thus the proposed new buildings can be instantly 'tested' in context when introduced to the elevation.

When the elevation drawing is prepared, selection can begin by a process of elimination, working with the larger format paintmakers' colour cards mentioned earlier in this chapter. For small-scale projects selection can simply take place while studying a shortlist of paint samples held against the site chart. During this stage, however, there are several considerations that should be taken into account. For instance, the question of a colour scheme's intended function; whether to camouflage or to contrast (a subject expanded on in the final chapter). During this phase, Lenclos devises two colour ranges drawn from paintmakers' colour cards against his 'chromatic palettes': one comprising harmonizing colours; another that complements those of the site. Against these new charts he then develops a range of contrasting colours which, as the former are intended for façades, will clearly define the smaller elements such as doors, frames and shutters, etc.

Another consideration is the quality of natural light on the site, since colour behaviour changes from one condition to another. For example, a colour which appears apt in the clear light of coastal or mountainous regions can appear quite wrong when seen under cloudy skies or through the haze of industrial pollution. The size of an area of colour is yet another factor affecting choice. Although difficult to predict accurately, the general rule holds that bright colours increase in brilliance with area, and pale versions tend to fade into insignificance when enlarged to architectural proportions. Furthermore, there is the important question of tonal value in relation to the orientation of a building; light colours help to brighten shadowed or shaded areas, while darker colours reduce the glare on planes bathed in strong sunlight.

Once a selection has been made, however, colours can be either painted on to the elevation drawing using gouache, or rendered with coloured pencils or crayons. An alternative technique is that of visualizing with coloured papers. This is extremely popular among both interior designers and architects, and is thoroughly recommended for the beginner. It involves the direct application of colours cut to shape from the larger paintmakers' samples or from

tion of representative colour charts. From these a collage of colour combinations—assembled as elevations from pre-painted paper sheets—present his proposals for a sympathetic architectural colour. COURTESY: JEAN-PHILIPPE LENCLOS

do-it-yourself equivalents painted in colour-matched gouache. Here, the elevation drawing acts as the basis for a collage—a fast technique that builds up the elevation in superimposed layers of coloured elements. The placing of one colour over another allows instant colour interaction and, prior to glueing down, an invaluable opportunity to try out optional colour schemes. This is yet another method employed by Lenclos. Figure **5.15** shows the range of mediums and techniques he uses within his complete sequence of design.

Two mediums often utilized as colouring agents in architectural graphics are felt- or fibre-tipped markers and dry-transfer colour sheets—each available in colours co-ordinated with the other. These both have advantages and disadvantages. On the one hand, markers are portable and instantaneous but, unless an extremely wide range is used, they tend to be unrelenting in their insensitivity to colour nuances. They are mainly employed for organizational purposes in the embryonic design stage. Dry-transfer sheets, on the other hand, require a painstaking application; they are usually incorporated into presentation orthographics in their opaque or transparent film form. Although unwieldy, the latter are widely used by architects when schematically colouring building concepts. These mediums are worthy of note simply because they bring evidence of colour thinking to the development of architectural ideas (**5.16**).

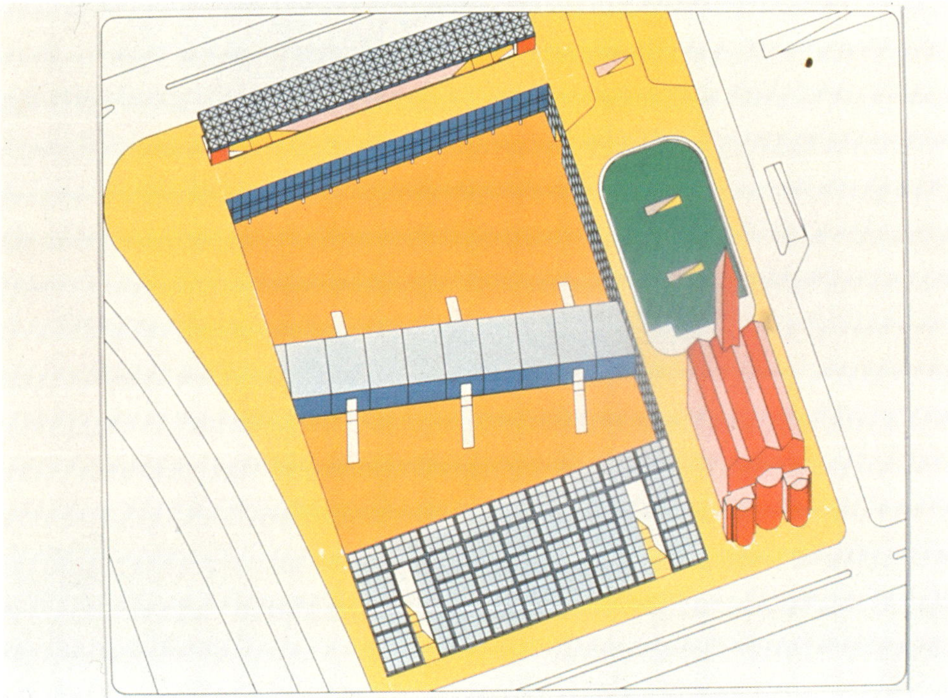

5.16 Presentation axonometric, Mathias Ungers. Although unwieldy as a colour medium, dry-transfer colour is widely used on architectural presentation drawings to introduce flat areas of descriptive colour, or to indicate functional zones schematically. However, its use in graphics to differentiate high-tech components has also influenced a stronger use of architectural colour in the environment at large.
COURTESY: MATHIAS UNGERS

5.17a and b Illinois library and garage models, Stanley Tigerman. The simple-to-construct scale block model provides the most reliable vehicle on which to finalize colour decisions destined for three-dimensional settings. Tigerman's maquettes for his Regional Library for the Blind and Physically Handicapped and its adjacent garage are built from cardboard, which is then laminated with pre-painted paper. COURTESY: STANLEY TIGERMAN

The most rewarding decision-making technique, however, is the use of the scale block model, as it can simulate colour dynamically along five dimensions, viz: hue, value (lightness) and chroma (saturation), plus time and angle of view. Cardboard block models are comparatively easy to construct, the quickest technique being the spray adhesive mounting or heatmounting of dyeline printed design elevations onto card before trace-cutting their silhouettes with a scalpel and glue-assembling on a baseboard. Rudimentary but useful models of existing buildings can also be constructed from elevations cut from cardboard boxes—their proportions inferred from sketches or photographs. Unlike presentation models, which occur exclusively at the end of the design process, block models do not concern themselves with small details or precision. Instead, they act as three-dimensional supports receiving trial colour proposals in either brush-applied pigment or that applied in the form of self-coloured or pre-painted papers, either before or after assembly.

The value of this technique is underlined by its widespread occurrence in the design of large- and small-scale buildings. For example, block models are a key design tool in the multifarious projects of Charles Moore—the maquette being particularly important to the development of his complex scheme for the Burns House. Also, Lenclos often transfers his ideas into 'the round', especially when dealing with larger forms such as the Chateau-Double apartments at Aix-en-Provence. When fine-tuning his primary hues for the Illinois Regional Library for the Blind and Physically Handicapped, Stanley Tigerman worked from simply constructed cardboard models scaled to represent the forms of both the main building and its separate garage unit (**5.17**).

5.18 Colours for Les Linandes, Cergy-Pontoise. A wall of ten acrylic and ten oil-based colours displayed on the site prior to their ultimate application by Jean-Philippe Lenclos. This was his means of testing their effect under the changing quality of local light conditions and, of course, of previewing public reaction. PHOTO: JEAN-PHILIPPE LENCLOS

Testing and communicating colour decisions

If disasters on a large scale are to be avoided, then some method of testing colours destined for external use is a vital facet of the selection process. The most useful is an *in situ* check on the perceptual effects of changes in colour intensity due to size, which may not have been predicted on colour chip, elevation drawing or model. This also allows a preview of the relative value levels of selected colours under the predominant lighting conditions together with the opportunity of gaining an impression of their appearance from a distance. This can be achieved by pre-painting a representative section of an existing façade to include wall, pipes, frames, doors, etc., using small samples of the actual paints intended for use. A variation of this method (and a technique capable of use on sites for proposed buildings) is that practised by Foster Meagher. Prior to handing his specification to the paint contractor, he paints a square metre of primed hardboard with the façade colour, using either the rough or smooth side of the hardboard, depending on which most resembles the texture of the wall surface. Stripes are then added and coloured to represent the smaller, vertical elements. The colour of projecting horizontal elements are represented on strips of hardboard attached at right angles to the former. This contraption is then placed against the house so that its paintwork receives light at the correct angle, and the result assessed in liaison with his client. A similar method was adopted by Lenclos for his twenty prescribed colours for the Les Linandes housing development. These were trial painted as vertical format panels with horizontal stripes on a blank wall in Cergy Pontoise. This exposure provided an outdoor test of his scheme on a large scale within the site context and allowed local residents the opportunity of experiencing them before their final application (**5.18**).

This type of public exposure begins to allow some participation in colour co-ordination by those who will have to live with it. Several participatory schemes have proved successful: for instance, the public display of architectural colour ranges for façades by Oscar Newman during his upgrading of Clason Point in New York; the similar but more persuasively motivated exposure of historic colours by Giovanni Brino and his team in Turin; and the award-winning scheme for Höchst, devised by German designer Gerhard Schweizer.

The latter project involved the selection of colours for a plasticized stucco together with paint colours for ornamental detailing on medieval façades. Deciding that the residents should take part in the scheme, Schweizer produced a twin-ringed colour wheel. Its inner wheel contained seven main façade colours, its outer counterpart seven four-colour displays of stronger colours plus black and white intended for half-timbering, ornamental detailing and doors and shutters, etc. (**5.19**). He then asked each resident in turn to choose their preferred façade colour, and to rotate the outer wheel until an

5.19 Colour wheels, Gerhard Schweizer. The inner and outer wheels contain two co-ordinated paint ranges devised by Schweizer for the walls and details of houses in the town of Höchst. From these, residents selected their individual schemes. The wheels are made from card and painted in gouache, colour-matched to the actual paints and pigments intended for use. COURTESY: GERHARD SCHWEIZER

acceptable combination was achieved. After initially selecting the full range of colours, Schweizer's role in this exercise was simply that of overall co-ordinator.

When block models are used in the development of colour for architecture, their existence allows proposals to be tested against their settings and the results to be communicated to clients in a format that is familiar. A photo-montage, for instance, is made by introducing a cut-out colour photograph of a model into a colour print made of the site. Another composite colour image is achieved by photographing a coloured model placed in front of a back-projected transparency of the site. Both techniques, however, require great skill and attention to details such as the integration of perspective, scale and direction of light. Also, both techniques are subject to colour distortion.

A direct method of producing composite transparencies or prints is found in the research work of Professor A. C. Hardy. He tests his proposals for attachment and detachment by photographing his painted models of farm buildings directly against their site. The model is held in an elevated position at some distance from the site by a wire that is driven into the ground. This is photographed after its relative scale and size have been determined through the viewfinder. The result can be quite stunning, conveying a most convincing simulation of the colour of a large architectural form when integrated with its site (**5.20**).

5.20 Model-setting photo-simulation technique. Professor A. C. Hardy's technique for producing composite colour photographs is simple to achieve. The model is supported on thin wire and fixed at a point from which, through a camera viewfinder, its scale appears compatible with that of its intended setting. To compensate for focal discrepancy, a Macro lens is used to photograph the resultant image. Figure 3.11 on page 47 illustrates the convincing effect of this technique.
COURTESY: A. C. HARDY

5.21 Public Office Building, Portland, Michael Graves. For architects such as Michael Graves, the colour-rendered elevation is a natural method of architectural visualization; his involvement with colour on the drawing board extends logically to realized buildings. For the beginner, a similar studio use of coloured design graphics is the first step in the development of an ability to deploy environmental colour with confidence. PHOTO: TED BICKFORD

The rendered elevation drawing, however, remains as the traditional means of communication throughout the design process and between designer and client and, together with information such as the hue, value (lightness) and chroma (saturation) notations of each prescribed colour, as the specification for the painter and contractor. In a sense, it is via the elevation drawing—more than any other mode of representation—that colour as an instrument of design has returned in proper measure to the visualization of the built form. Its return is celebrated in the graphic work of all those designers mentioned here, and in the widely published graphics of architects such as Ricardo Bofill, Robert Stern and Michael Graves, it achieves the status of art in its own right (**5.21**).

In conclusion we now turn to a review of the functions of colour.

6 COLOUR FUNCTIONS IN ARCHITECTURE

The use of colour in architectural design has never been without its evangelists or its practitioners. One of its German advocates was the architect Bruno Taut, who, in the twenties, battled for environmental colour while a Councillor for Magdeburg, and later when he built his low-cost housing areas in Berlin. One of them, the Uncle Tom's Cabin estate (recently restored to its original reds and yellows by Helge Pitz and Winifried Brenne) used colour decisions based on a complex musical harmony. Taut had observed that in an old Magdeburg street which was half painted and half left grey, it was possible on a rainy day to see how the painted section possessed a 'plastic and truly material life', while the grey part seemed a 'disturbing abstract ghost'. Although many see Le Corbusier's work in their mind's eye as blanched, as a result of consistently achromatic publication, he echoed Taut when he wrote in the following decade: 'A fundamental truth: man needs colour.'

Decorative colour

Although architectural polychromy can perform many environmental functions and operate on various levels of consciousness in the observer, perhaps its most obvious is to attract the attention. This function is illustrated in the use of paint on the Van Wezel Performing Arts Hall in Sarasota, Florida. Its managing director, Curtis Haug, explains: 'One of the smartest things the architect did was to have this building painted purple. Because of its colour and unique design we average about four thousand visitors a month who drive off the main highway just to see what the building is.' The Hall was, in fact, designed by Frank Lloyd Wright and built after his death by the Taliesin Foundation; the colour—a pale violet—was actually chosen by his wife (**6.1**).

Such a response to this particular hue is interesting because within the now wider acceptance of more varied architectural colour, the results of research programmes such as that by Lars Sivik in Sweden have indicated a singular dislike for the use of pale violet in the environment. However, whether fact or fiction, the rarity of purples and violets on buildings has not been due entirely to preference but to its fugitiveness in paint and in most materials. One might therefore hazard a guess that the attraction of this colour in Sarasota could have something to do with its rarity. However, Haug recounts that when the Hall was painted there was much local controversy—which later subsided into acceptance. He also suggests that when the building was due for repainting some time ago he felt sure there would have been even more controversy if the pale violet had been changed to some other colour!

6.1 (preceding page) Van Wezel Performing Arts Hall, Florida. The extraordinary pulling power of this lilac and white combination is remarkable. Attracting thousands of curious visitors, the Hall now boasts a bevy of purple-clad hostesses, who run guided tours around the building which, incidentally, is painted purple on the inside and filled with purple seats. It was designed by Frank Lloyd Wright and the colours chosen by his wife. PHOTO: TOM PORTER

Decorative colour on dwellings is often used by the occupant as a sort of signature which, apart from acting as a protective layer, describes personality, status and territory. In extreme cases one can find each side of a boundary drainpipe in terraced housing painted in the emblematic colours of joint ownership. Creative expression can be found in the meticulous painting of every façade element, sometimes extending to the elaboration of individual bricks and mortar joints. More subtle changes can be found in high-density areas where colour and texture play tandem roles in defining areas of territorial space. For example, in combination with surface treatments in Oxford's medieval backstreets mellow colour-washes not only accentuate gentle surface undulations but subtly demarcate individual façades and help communicate differences between 'public' and 'private' zones. Similarly, in Greek villages—where a colour identity is restricted to the woodwork of doors and shutters—the annual ritual of limewashing houses and pavements acts as a kind of rebirth. Paint redefines the close working relationship of inter-personal spaces, with progressive layers of pigment softening the corners of form and welding vertical to horizontal (**6.2**).

6.2 Aegean village, Greece. As a result of countless annual applications of whitewash, Greek island villages are transformed into a kind of architectural confectionery—paint appears almost translucent under the sparkling Aegean sunlight. Limewash is used on walls, roofs, steps and street paving and is relieved only by the distinctive emerald greens and turquoise blue-greens of oil-based paintwork applied to protect the woodwork of doors, frames and balustrades. PHOTO: ROY BARRIS

Symbolic colour

One aspect of decoration is the use of colour to symbolize concepts which lie beyond the architecture it adorns. This has already been discussed in the buildings of Michael Graves, Paolo Portoghesi and Robert Stern, Post-Modernists who use colour as a direct form of symbolism which makes references to nature and the elements. Their applications continue a colour tradition rooted in the past, beginning when man first reddened his body and later brought the colours of the planets, fields and sky to his buildings. In the modern environment, such a direct association of ideas can be found in

6.2

the blazing red of Gunnar Birkert's fire station and in the aqua blue of the Pacific Design Centre by Cesar Pelli & Associates.

Another facet of colour symbolism which finds its way into architecture is the indirect association of ideas using colour symbols which, unlike the universal association of 'red' with 'fire', carry more abstract meanings. For instance, white (used as a symbol of mourning in China) represents the incorruptibility of the White House; there is a 'red light' association in the pink-painted façades of a Pigalle nightclub; and a revolutionary connotation

6.3 House in San Francisco. Any study of the symbolic use of red in the built environment will elicit a wealth of both direct and indirect associations of ideas. For example, the occupants of this house, lawyers Joseph Rhine and Michael Kennedy, were branded Communists when involved in the defence of Timothy Leary and Angela Davis during litigation against the Free Speech Movement at Berkeley. As a riposte, they symbolically redecorated their offices in an emotive red paint. PHOTO: © by MORLEY BAER FROM *Painted Ladies*

in the orange-red of the Maxim Gorky Elementary School in Nanterre, France. There is also the defiant red on the San Francisco law office redecorated by its occupants when, after counselling members of the Free Speech Movement, they were accused of being left-wing (**6.3**).

Another aspect of symbolism is the way in which architectural colour is used to fashion a building either as part of the landscape or to stand out from it as an environmental focal point. This choice has been present throughout history, from the time when man lived as part of the landscape in caves, but also built temples which he deliberately and symbolically placed on artificial sites. Updated, we can see the same symbolism today if we compare a Le Corbusier house in a green field with a carefully sited Frank Lloyd Wright house of the same colour as the earth on which it stands.

Colour attachment

A common function of environmental colour, therefore, is to help blend objects into their background—the opposite of attracting attention. This process of 'attachment' through colour came to the fore in the development and application of camouflage during World War Two. Its object was to visually break up the silhouettes of industrial forms using the principle by which animals and insects 'borrow' pattern and colour from their habitats as a means of escaping the notice of predators. Remnants of gigantic earth-coloured supergraphics can still be detected today on the outside of many factories such as the British Leyland plant in Oxford, which during the war was used for building aeroplanes rather than motor cars, and was therefore a prime target. From ground level the purpose of the broad irregular patches of mainly lightish green, lightish khaki and black paint is difficult to establish. The point is that when viewed from the air by an alien bomber pilot, camouflage made the plant much more difficult to identify. Essentially, camouflage against aerial views depends upon texture to reduce shine, and on strong contrasts between lighter and darker values to disrupt shape and alter give-away shadows. Textured paint was also occasionally used to disguise factory roofs by imitating the size and pattern of terraced housing in the vicinity (**6.4**).

6.4 Chimney at British Leyland plant, Cowley, Oxford. The very existence of this chimney—together with that of its fading paintwork—is testament to the wartime success of camouflage: contrived patchwork patterns of earth colour serving to intervene in the recognition of industrial forms from the air. PHOTO: ALAN COLEMAN (IVOR FIELDS PHOTOGRAPHIC)

Although efforts to blend architecture into its surroundings can never entirely succeed, the principles used in camouflage are relevant. Much of Professor A. C. Hardy's work on 'attachment' reaches exactly the same conclusion. Namely, the reduction of shine by a use of matt paints; the break-up of large or directional shapes using different colours culled from the site area; and, most important, a firm control on the levels of value in order to help shift visual emphasis elsewhere in the immediate setting.

Often, however, the architect decides to select just one predominant

6.5 Warehouse for Modern Art Glass, Thamesmead. Norman Foster describes his colour philosophy thus: 'The juxtaposition of buildings in the landscape can be of two kinds: imposition of the man-made object on the landscape, or a careful integration of a man-made object which is more akin to the earth—either hollowed out of it or blending in as part of the natural landscape.' PHOTO: JOHN DONAT

6.6 Herman Miller factory, Bath. The opposite of exuberant decoration is the use of colour to make environmental objects as inconspicuous as possible. This stratagem, known for ages in the animal kingdom, was used by the Farrell/Grimshaw Partnership to reduce the intrusion of their factory unit in a city-based industrial park. PHOTO: JO REID AND JOHN PECK

colour from the setting to which his building responds. Various attempts to merge rigorously modern forms with their environment have been made, from the concrete of Peter Womersley's Nuffield Transplantation Surgery Unit in Edinburgh to I. M. Pei's Upper Atmosphere Observatory in Colorado, both tinted to act as a chromatic consensus, of local brickwork and Rocky Mountain stone respectively. There is also Richard Rogers' chlorophyll-coloured O.U.P. Fragrances factory planted in the green of the Surrey countryside, and Norman Foster's appeal to the heavens from his sky-blue warehouse for Modern Art Glass which sits amidst the legislated industrial greyness of Thamesmead (**6.5**). When designing their factory for Herman Miller in Bath, architects Farrell and Grimshaw had pigment injected into its G.R.P. (glass reinforced plastic) cladding in a somewhat vain attempt to key its glossy shell into the mellowness of local stonework (**6.6**). With similar purpose, many stuccoed façades of buildings in older High Streets are coated with exterior paints that mimic their stone-finished counterparts in the locality or, if these are non-existent, paint is used to simulate different materials which could not be afforded.

This kind of colour keying is advocated by Jean-Philippe Lenclos, who, except in extraordinary circumstances, is opposed to the arbitrary and indiscriminate use of colour for its own sake. After his thorough investigation of a

6.7 Brixham harbour, Devon. This communal orchestration of coastal architectural colour seems entirely fitting to its seaside setting. As if to celebrate their confrontation with the sea, houses descend from the upper levels of predominantly achromatic façades down to a climax of more saturated, contrasting and variegated colours on the harbour frontage. PHOTO: JOHN DRAPER

site, he selects architectural pilot colours that make direct reference to prominent geological or vegetal colours in the terrain, to applied paints and the colours of building materials in the immediate setting, and to a consideration of self-coloured materials for the building itself. Urban settings will produce colour selections liable to be discordant in the countryside, while colour schemes found suitable for seaside architecture or for brick and slate townhouses are not likely to be in keeping with the stonework of village cottages (**6.7**). Lenclos also makes his colour decisions against a scale of integration. At one end lies the decision to key a building to its surroundings; at the other lies the opposite aim of colour used to detach the building from its surroundings (**6.8**).

6.8 Degrees of colour attachment. This drawing by Jean-Philippe Lenclos illustrates the scale of integration he considers when prescribing colour for the built environment. He suggests that these are the options that present themselves whenever a building is to be painted. At one end of the scale lies a decision to apply a uniform colour sympathetic to surroundings as a means of making a building less conspicuous. At the other end lies a stratagem that introduces a surface pattern which does not submit to the contours of form. He explains that his range of options is entirely biological. Nature provides a universal source of reference, from the conformity of leaf-mimicking moths to the random dappling of cows in the pasture. COURTESY: JEAN-PHILIPPE LENCLOS

Colour detachment

Colour detachment occurs when colour is used simply to celebrate architecture and intensify our experience of it; it is active rather than passive as the many examples mentioned in previous chapters have shown. Here, colour is used 'sculpturally' in order to underline architectural expression for its own sake, or is selectively deployed to attract the eye to features considered worthy of such attention. The idea of strong colours, exploiting non-traditional finishes, to target forms against neutral backgrounds is part of a Modern Movement usage. In the late forties, Marcel Breuer had extolled the virtues of architectural primary colours set against white and grey as befitting a radical architecture related to the machine age. As part of this tradition, the man-made object functions aggressively in opposition to nature—a decision which sets a Le Corbusier white house in a green field. Le Corbusier also loved to use a detached and sculptural primary colour against his external planes of white. Typical of his work is the insertion of strong hues into indentations in his buildings to scoop out space in colour seemingly left behind after the overall modelling of the form. More recently, Norman Foster, another architect who tends to use strong colour in and on his buildings, describes his predilection for colour as an intuitive preference stemming from eye-catching advertisements and contractor's machinery. When explaining this aspect of his design group's attitude, he said: 'We enjoy the visual excitement of the juxtaposition of vivid colours and their effect in the landscape.'

The concept of detachment, therefore, usually follows the designer's desire to create a new atmosphere with colour; a bright scheme tending to express architectural diversity, gaiety and excitement. By rejecting conformity to setting, this approach seeks to express the essential character of the building. Colour is used to discriminate different materials, to define form and volume, their impressions often intensified when the colours used contrast with surroundings. Games are also played with scale and proportion. Colours are arranged vertically to increase apparent height; when arranged horizontally, width is emphasized. When the lines, planes and openings of a building are described in contrasting colours, the scale of the built form is more easily read from close at hand and from a distance.

The growth of a raw concrete architecture brought with it the need to soften its impact. The widespread painting of concrete occurs mainly in France and Germany where, particularly in the latter country, tradition tends to associate unpainted surfaces with 'unfinished' surfaces. Here, colour decisions are based on certain premises. Schemes involving a single colour are avoided because large-scale areas in monochrome can induce an impression of the monolithic, or are considered to be boring. Overly complicated schemes involving aggressively extreme colour contrast are also shunned in

6.9 Apartments at Bergramen, Westphalia. This is typical of the award-winning work of German colourist Friedrich Ernst von Garnier. His colour schemes exploit the range of intensity and clearness of single or paired families of hue in the provision of 'identity' and 'similarity' harmonies. These are applied for the sole purpose of 'personalizing' architecture, paint being applied to obliterate the large areas of concrete he finds so aggressive in the modern urban environment. PHOTO: FRIEDRICH ERNST V. GARNIER

favour of rich colours arranged to follow form in 'identity' or 'similarity' harmonies employing stepped progressions of hue, chroma and value. A common feature of schemes for larger buildings is the careful arrangement of tonal value to avoid top-heaviness; darker, heavier values are confined to lower levels, acting as 'plinths' which visually anchor buildings to their ground-plane (**6.9**).

Supergraphic colour (colourful camouflage)

During the last two decades, the sheer size of architecture also became subject to a colour application which, seeking to fragment scale and mass, pursued detachment in another way. In describing bold patterns to visually erode an impression of form, supergraphic colour came to reject both site and support. It has obvious links with wall painting but, more interestingly, has roots in a celebratory community art form which flourishes spasmodically. During America's Bicentennial, for example, fire hydrants everywhere became transformed into comic personalities under the paint brushes of schoolchildren. Also, in Britain's Jubilee Year, patriotic flecks of red, white and blue paint transformed streets and villages into 'pointilliste' Union Jacks. Meanwhile, artists on both sides of the Atlantic in search of more ambitious 'canvases' turned to the decorative coloration of industrial and environmental landmarks such as chimneys, pylons and water towers. Competitions were launched to encourage a more widespread use of colour, including facelifting prescriptions for the more blighted inner urban areas.

Supergraphics have become an all-out attack on the appearance of form—often by the architect himself. For its initial inspiration it drew from the more obvious Pop Art references: arrows, bull's eyes, stripes, numerals and letterforms. What followed was a return to a form of camouflage but this time using nets of brilliant colour splashes to show off an ambiguity between architectural form and its skin of paint. Much of this development has proved superficial but at its best it has become an architecture in itself (**6.10**).

6.10 Ni-Ban-Kahn, Tokyo, Minoru Takeyama. The fashion for architectural supergraphics represents the architect's answer to wall painting. Drawing from Pop Art symbolism, stripes, arrows and letterforms, etc. have been magnified to building proportions as a means of breaking up blank exterior planes, in some cases used paradoxically to change a three-dimensional impression of physical form. PHOTO: MINORU TAKEYAMA

One of the most unusual applications was undertaken in 1974 when sculptor Alexander Calder redirected his colour expertise from the urban scale of his city sculpture and the dynamics of mobiles to the aerodynamics of Tristar jets. As part of Braniff International's multicoloured fleet he designed livery for five carriers. Calder's supergraphics break with traditional streamlining (but remain within a long tradition of brightly painted forms of transportation) by creating colourful flying sculpture with echoes of the heraldic camouflage of 'Blue Max' biplanes. As if to emphasize his humorous send-up of gallery art, Calder personally and publicly signed each aeroplane, thereby completing a commission which resulted in Braniff inviting future passengers to 'Fly in a Work of Art' (**6.11**).

6.11 *Flying Colours.* Alexander Calder's design for the livery of Braniff International's flagship. COURTESY: BRANIFF INTERNATIONAL

Calder
N1805

The architectural monument to supergraphics is found in the Nanterre district near Paris. Here, Fabio Rieti has created a startling design on the surface of eight tower blocks designed by architect Emile Aillaud. Known collectively as the 'Candles', the mosaic skin of their rounded forms appears to mimic cloudfilled skies while others simulate the contours and colours of earth and foliage. In making these references to natural elements, however, Rieti is quick to deny any attempt at attachment; quite the opposite, for his intention was to create a surrealist Magritte environment (**6.12**).

Rieti's use of coloured shapes completely at variance with their supporting architectural form does, however, illustrate the essence of an approach practised by many European colourists. This involves a colourful 'camouflage' using broken areas of brilliant colour to fragment a monumental mass (the very approach used by Lenclos for the overbearing façades of the Campagne-Lévèque housing). It is a philosophy which, when a building is considered out of scale with its setting or a site considered devoid of colour identity, promotes the injection of strong colour as a 'humanizing' element which will introduce a sense of place.

Lenclos' use of more saturated colour is almost invariably applied in industrial settings. His work at the Acièrie Solmer Steel plant at Fos-sur-mer

6.12 Tower blocks in Nanterre, France. The original idea of colouring these apartment towers with vertical stripes which gradually darkened as they entered the 'folds' of the forms was abandoned. Instead, colourist Fabio Rieti felt that the area needed more wit to combat the solemnity which is often the lot of modern environments. PHOTO: PATRICE GOULET

6.13 Crane at Acièrie Solmer Steel plant, Fos-sur-mer. The Acièrie Solmer industrial zone occupies a desert region which approximates an area the size of Paris. Within the site roam five gigantic cranes, and, as a member of the Urbame design group, Jean-Philippe Lenclos assigned his colours so that each could be singled out from its identical counterparts at a great distance.
PHOTO: JEAN-PHILIPPE LENCLOS

near Marseilles includes five gigantic cranes for which he prescribed colours to function in three different ways: first, to make them clearly visible in a polluted atmosphere, and to give each an identity (prior to repainting they had been a uniform grey); second, to fragment their huge size, the differences among them being indicated by a predominant pilot colour (afterwards he learned that each was given a nickname by operatives); third, to assign different colours to each of the cranes' components in order to code what was safe from what was dangerous (**6.13**).

Colour coding

The indexing through colour of obstacles and hazards in machine environments is another branch of detachment; an eye-catching function transferred by designers to the other components of their architecture. This function emanates from the code for pipe identification together with the safety colours (**6.14**). This 'language' of colour—devised to safeguard users of workshops, plants and offices—has provided the point of departure from which many architects have made their first excursions into the realms of very strong colours. Any study of its many external applications, however,

![ICI logo] **Dulux** *Pipe identification and safety colours*

Pipe identification

Water Pipes	Basic identification colour 12 D 45 Sherwood
Water type	**Optional coding colours - BS4800 reference/Dulux Trade Gloss colour**
cooling	White
drinking	18 E 53 Regatta
boiler feed	04 D 45 Monarch/White/04 D 45 Monarch
condensate	04 D 45 Monarch/14 E 53 Verona/04 D 45 Monarch
chilled	White/14 E 53 Verona/White
central heating above 100 C	04 D 45 Monarch/18 E 53 Regatta/04 D 45 Monarch
central heating below 100 C	18 E 53 Regatta/04 D 45 Monarch/18E53 Regatta
cold from storage	White/18 E 53 Regatta/White
hot supply	White/04 D 45 Monarch/White
hydraulic power	04 C 33 Shell
sea/river untreated	Basic colour only
fire extinguishing	04 E 53 Poppy

A

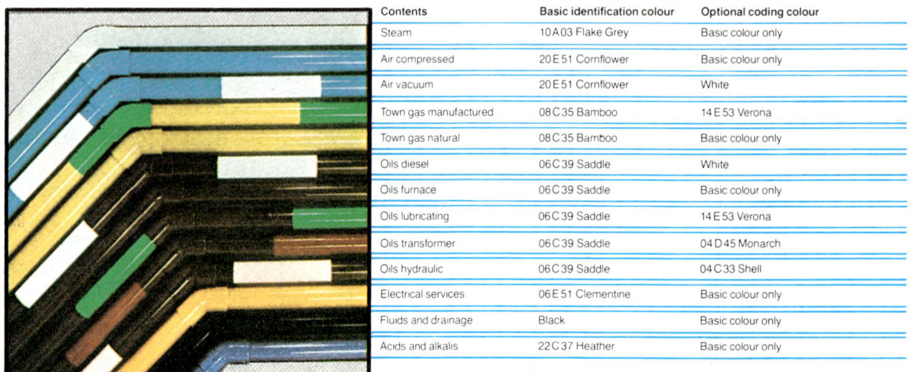

Contents	Basic identification colour	Optional coding colour
Steam	10 A 03 Flake Grey	Basic colour only
Air compressed	20 E 51 Cornflower	Basic colour only
Air vacuum	20 E 51 Cornflower	White
Town gas manufactured	08 C 35 Bamboo	14 E 53 Verona
Town gas natural	08 C 35 Bamboo	Basic colour only
Oils diesel	06 C 39 Saddle	White
Oils furnace	06 C 39 Saddle	Basic colour only
Oils lubricating	06 C 39 Saddle	14 E 53 Verona
Oils transformer	06 C 39 Saddle	04 D 45 Monarch
Oils hydraulic	06 C 39 Saddle	04 C 33 Shell
Electrical services	06 E 51 Clementine	Basic colour only
Fluids and drainage	Black	Basic colour only
Acids and alkalis	22 C 37 Heather	Basic colour only

B

Safety colours

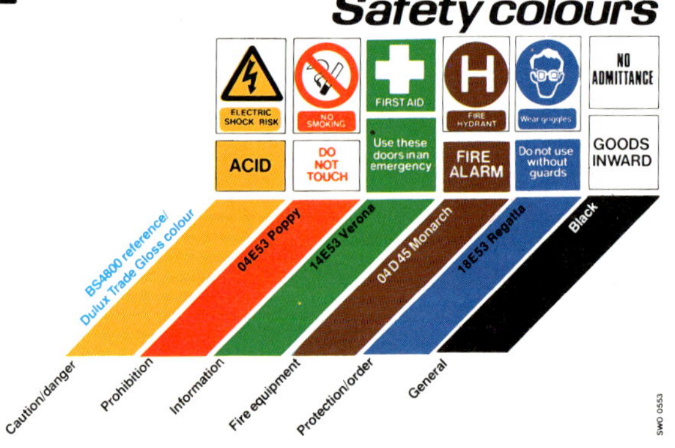

C

reveals that its relationship to established meanings in industrial coding is sham. Behind claims that their schemes are 'industrial', 'coded' or 'factory-planned', is a straightforward enjoyment in diagramming complex structures, together with the creation of aesthetically stimulating compositions.

The control of contrast between hues lies at the essence of 'indexing' a building. It also draws from the easily recognizable primary and intermediate hues, but this does not mean that forms are merely blasted with saturated colour. Designers of the better examples of this genre have questioned 'which red?', 'which blue?' and 'which yellow?', for within each region there are many variants. Again, decisions on colour tones are extremely important. As well as their discriminatory uses, darker colours are generally applied to support elements and lighter colours used for the suspended or supported. This colour use is illustrated in the coloration of the metal parts of a meat-processing factory designed by Osmo Mikkonen and Pasi Raevaara in Finland (**6.15**). Two other examples, this time in concrete, are found in

6.14 a, b and c Pipe identification and safety colours. Charts A and B are based on the British Standard 1710, *Identification of Pipelines*, 1975. They represent the confidence-giving source from which many designers have devised colour schemes for the diagramming of architectural elements in both interiors and exteriors. The basic identification colours, which indicate the essential nature of the contents, are applied along the length of pipework, and in 150 mm wide bands. Optional coding colours indicate a pipe's precise contents, and are superimposed on the basic colour in 100 mm wide bands at strategic positions. The safety colours are shown in Chart C. In January 1981, a European Economic Community directive required all safety signposting to comply with a uniform system of symbols and colours. COURTESY: IMPERIAL CHEMICAL INDUSTRIES, LTD.

6.15 Karjakunta factory, Riihimaki, Finland. A steel and glass factory by architects Osmo Mikkonen and Pasi Raevaara which required painting against corrosion. The steel structure was coded a dark blue for columns and beams with a light blue for surface panels. Against the predominance of these two 'reference' blues, orange was selected for shutters and chimney, with red for mechanized traffic doors and yellow for pedestrian access doors. COURTESY: OSMO MIKKONEN

Thailand where Jumsai Associates employ a practical coding on their School for the Blind (**6.16**) and Bangkok apartments (**6.17**). Both buildings use painted elements as a means of distinguishing assembled and non-assembled components—a system used throughout Thailand.

These examples demonstrate a rule common in fine art when handling the more saturated colours or, for that matter, any other combination. It is that one should consider the size and balance of colours—selecting schemes which centre on a dominant pilot hue. Against this, other colours will then play a supporting role in the visual field. This is because a juxtaposition of strong colours of similar tonal value or chromatic strength can be self-defeating, because of the equal claims for attention of colours of similar area, lightness and saturation.

The claims for these wider and richer applications of colour contained within this book are manifold. Some architects and designers suggest that its considered dispersal will reduce vandalism in urban settings; others suggest that in industrial settings its careful prescription might help increase levels of production. Whatever the speculation, however, colour is a potential means of influencing people's reactions to their visual environment. In the hands of the professional designer it can regulate the perception of buildings; in the hands of the occupiers it is a way of involving themselves at first-hand in the articulation of their habitat. Colour may not be the complete answer to our urban ills but it can bring some lightheartedness, some real benefit and, more important, some vitality to our everyday experience of space.

Meanwhile, the surface of built form is comprised of a seeming multitude of different materials some of which, for their protection against weather and corrosion, require a preservative coating which can also serve as a vehicle for colour (**6.18**). Very often an adventurous application of colour is misinformed and its success or failure too much a matter of chance. The tendency, therefore, is to play safe and to follow convention, however dull. If this book encourages architects and designers to give serious attention to the many ways colour can improve the environment we live in, it will have succeeded in its purpose. We cannot enjoy colour at its best if we neglect or fear to use it!

6.16 Bangkok School for the Blind, Thailand. This is a detail of a low-cost building designed by the Thai group, Sumet Jumsai Associates. Its concrete structural frame was transported in pieces and assembled on site. Jumsai's application of a 'colour-coded' paintwork represents a further example of those designers who have borrowed from the functional language used for the marking of industrial hazards and the identifying of certain equipment. COURTESY: SUMET JUMSAI

6.17 Bangkok apartments. This is a further example of the colour-coding function in the design work of Sumet Jumsai Associates, this time on an apartment complex with a rooftop penthouse. A strong colour combination comprises white for wall and balcony panels braced by a blue, green and ochre to diagram assembled and non-assembled concrete elements in a structure of prestressed beams and precast floor units with columns cast *in situ*. COURTESY: SUMET JUMSAI

6.18 a and b Acièrie Solmer Steel plant before and after painting. Essentially, paint functions as a protective skin—a layer of suspended particles of solid pigment which preserves corrosive materials. But colour can also create changing backgrounds to human activity; it can, as in this case, bring a humanizing element to the often inhuman scale of industrial forms. PHOTOS: JEAN-PHILIPPE LENCLOS

BIBLIOGRAPHY AND INDEX

BIBLIOGRAPHY

Ambasz, E. *The Architecture of Luis Barragán,* Museum of Modern Art, New York, 1976.

Baldwin, H. *Colour on Buildings: 1500–1800,* Oxford Polytechnic, Department of Architecture, 1978.

Birren, F. *Light, Color and Environment,* Van Nostrand Reinhold, New York, 1969.

Birren, F. *Principles of Color,* Van Nostrand Reinhold, New York, 1969.

Brino, G. 'Colour in Turin', *Domus,* No 602, Jan. 1980.

Brino, G., & Rosso, F. *Colore e Cittá—Il Piano del Colore di Torino 1800–1850,* Idea Editions, Milan, 1980.

Broadbent, G. 'The Road to Xanadu and Beyond', *Progressive Architecture,* Sept. 1975.

Chocron, I. *Color Natural,* Ediciones del Grupo Montana, Caracas, 1970.

Davey, P. 'Factory, Castle Park, Nottingham', *The Architectural Review,* Dec. 1980.

Faulkner, W. *Architecture and Color,* Wiley-Interscience, New York, 1972.

Gloag, H. L., & Gold, M. J. *Colour Coordination Handbook,* Her Majesty's Stationery Office, London, 1978.

Goodman, S. 'Colour', Oxford Polytechnic, Department of Architecture, 1973.

Küppers, H. *Color: Origins, Systems, Uses,* Van Nostrand Reinhold, New York, 1972.

Larsen, M., & Pomada, E. *Painted Ladies: Those Resplendent Victorians,* E. P. Dutton, New York, 1978.

Lenclos, J.-P. 'France: How to Paint Industry', *Domus,* No 568, March 1977.

Lenclos, J.-P. 'La Méthode du Rythme et des Tonalités', *Architecture Intérieure-Crée,* 1979.

Marx, E. *The Contrast of Colors,* Van Nostrand Reinhold, New York, 1973.

McKean, J. M. 'Rainbow House', *Building Design,* June 1980.

Miller, N., et al., 'Colour in Architecture', *AIA Journal,* Oct. 1978.

Moon, P., & Spencer, D. E. 'Geometric Formulation of Classical Colour Harmony', *Journal of the Optical Society of America,* 1944.

Pavey, D., et al., *Colour,* Marshall Editions Limited, London, 1980.

Porter, T. 'A Taste for Colour', *The Architect,* Mar. 1977.

Porter, T., & Mikellides, B. *Colour for Architecture,* Studio Vista, London, 1976.

Porter T., & Mikellides, B. 'Language of Colour', *Designer,* Jan. 1977.

Portoghesi, P. 'Colour in Town', *Domus,* No 602, Jan. 1980.

Prizeman, J. *Your House—The Outside View,* Hutchinson, London, 1975.

INDEX

Numbers in italics refer to pages with illustrations